TEACHER DEVELOPMENT SERIES
Series Editor: Andy Hargreaves

THOUGHTFUL TEACHING

THOUGHTFUL TEACHING

Christopher M. Clark

Teachers College
Columbia University
New York and London

Published in the United States of America by
Teachers College Press, Columbia University,
1234 Amsterdam Ave., New York, N.Y. 10027 USA

Published in Great Britain by Cassell, London

Cataloging-in-Publication Data available through the Library of Congress

ISBN: 0-8077-3502-7

Typeset by York House Typographic Ltd, London
Manufactured in Great Britain

99 98 97 96 95   1 2 3 4 5

To our children: Chris, Jr, Tryn Rose, Martin, Daniel
and Victoria, who have taught me much of what
I know of thoughtful teaching.

Contents

PART Four CULTIVATING THOUGHTFUL TEACHING

Series Editor's Introduction

In Britain and Australia, they call it teaching. In the United States and Canada, they call it instruction. Whatever terms we use, we have come to realize in recent years that the teacher is the ultimate key to educational change and school improvement. The restructuring of schools, the composition of national and provincial curricula, the development of benchmark assessments – all these things are of little value if they do not take the teacher into account. Teachers don't merely deliver the curriculum. They develop, define it and reinterpret it too. It is what teachers think, what teachers believe and what teachers do at the level of the classroom that ultimately shapes the kind of learning that young people get. Growing appreciation of this fact is placing working with teachers and understanding teaching at the top of our research and improvement agendas.

For some reformers, improving teaching is mainly a matter of developing better teaching methods, of improving instruction. Training teachers in new classroom management skills, in active learning, co-operative leaning, one-to-one counselling and the like is the main priority. These things are important, but we are also increasingly coming to understand that developing teachers and improving their teaching involves more than giving them new tricks. We are beginning to recognize that, for teachers, what goes on inside the classroom is closely related to what goes on outside it. The quality, range and flexibility of teachers' classroom work are closely tied up with their professional growth – with the way that they develop as people and as professionals.

Teachers teach in the way they do not just because of the skills they have or have not learned. The ways they teach are also grounded in their backgrounds, their biographies, in the kinds of teachers they have become. Their careers – their hopes and dreams, their opportunities and aspirations, or the frustration of these things – are also important for teachers' colleagues – either as supportive communities who work together in pursuit of common goals and continuous improvement, or as individuals working in isolation, with the insecurities that sometimes brings.

As we are coming to understand these wider aspects of teaching and teacher development, we are also beginning to recognize that much more, than pedagogy, instruction or teaching method is at stake. Teacher development, teachers' careers, teachers' relations with their colleagues, the conditions of status, reward and leadership under which they work – all these affect the quality of what they do in the classroom.

This international series, Teacher Development, brings together some of the very best current research and writing on these aspects of teachers' lives and work. The books in the series seek to understand the wider dimensions of teachers' work, the depth of teachers' knowledge and the resources of biography and experience on which it draws, the ways that teachers' work roles and responsibilities are changing as we restructure our schools, and so forth. In this sense, the books in the series are written for those who are involved in research on teaching, those who work in intial and in-service teacher education, those who lead and administer teachers, those who work with teachers and, not least, teachers themselves.

This book, by on of the world's most accomplished researchers of teacher thinking, addresses the elegantly framed issue of 'Thoughtful Teaching'. The most casual glance at the book's contents will reveal that the title has a clever and apt double meaning.

One the one hand, Christopher Clark vividly elaborates how teaching is full of thinking; rigorous cognitive thinking full of planning, judgement, decision-making and deliberation. Bringing together a rich tradition of research that he and his colleagues have spearheaded over the years, Clark explores the sophistication and complexity of teachers' judgements. Teachers' do not follow the narrowly rational, linear plans of curriculum objectives or administrative preferences, but make decisions according to their passion and enthusiasm, and to the opportunities and constraints of the moment, of what teachers experience here and now. It is so important to highlight these characteristics of teacher thinking. Educational reform in the shape of outcomes-based education, still presumes that teaches can somehow begin designing their curriculum with abstract outcomes, then move to the details of their content later in a smooth, linear fashion. Yet my own work on teachers enthusiastically committed to integrated studies and also trying to make sense of common learning outcomes, begin with their own sense of what will ignite learning and engagement in their own students and brainstorm content and method from there. Only later do they revisit prescribed outcomes to check what they've missed. Teachers plan best in these more spontaneous an emotionally engaged ways with their children vividly in mind, but still feel guilty they are not planning in relation to outcomes 'properly'. Clark's excellent account of the non-linear but sophisticated nature of teacher thinking might help disabuse teachers and other is of these misconceptions about proper planning and relieve them of some of the burden of their guilt that they are failing to implement outcomes appropriately.

For Christopher Clark, teaching is also thoughtful as a second sense. It is considerate and kindly. Teaching is an emotional and a moral profession, not just a technical, cognitive one. Throughout this book he describes teachers who are thoughtful in this way – in his own vivid case descriptions, and as the father of an autistic and epileptic child. Christopher Clark's book is a moving book as well as a meaningful one. It is written from the heart and through the head, bringing together feeling and thinking in his own writing in the ways he clearly values for teachers.

In *Descartes' Error*, Antonio Damasio brilliantly shows that

> 'reason may not be as pure as most of us think it is or wish it were, that emotions and feeling may not be intruders in the bastion of reason at all: they may be enmeshed in its networks, for worse *and* for better'.

> (Damasio, A.R., *Descartes' Error: Emotion, Reason and the Human Brain,* New York, Grosset/Putnam, 1994, p.xii).

Clark's elegant analysis of teaching in experience, example and research shows how thoughtful teaching depends on this kind of synthesis of reason and emotion, feeling and thinking. He beautifully depicts how thoughtful so much teaching is, even in its most seemingly unremarkable manifestation. And he advocates that we should all aspire to making teaching more thoughtful still. *Thoughtful Teaching* is itself a profoundly thoughtful book. It will make you think and feel about teaching differently.

Andy Hargreaves
Ontario Institute for Studies in Education, Toronto.
April 1995

Acknowledgements

A circle of good and thoughtful people provided me with support and encouragement in the writing and rewriting of this book. I am greatly indebted to Andy Hargreaves who proposed the book, convinced me of its worth, and reassured me when my doubts threatened the project. In addition, Naomi Roth, publisher at Cassell, provided support from the beginning. My wife, Tryn Clark, generously provided encouragement and an unswerving sense of the potential importance of this work, especially for those sections concerning the moral dimensions of teaching.

Susan Florio-Ruane, Michal Zellermayer, Robert J. Yinger, Frances Rust, D. Jean Clandinin, Eliot W. Eisner, Miriam Ben-Peretz, Gunnar Handal, Karen Jensen, Sverker Lindblad, Anna Neumann, David Hunt, Rolf Dubs, Lauren C. Pfeiffer, Lily Bilelli, F. Michael Connelly, Steve Yelon, Karen Noordhoff, Grace Grant, and Sigrun Gudmundsdottir read parts of the manuscript, pushed me gently to clarify and condense, and saw lace where I saw only holes. This book and I have also benefited from the many thoughtful teachers and students I have had the pleasure of working with and learning from in classes, in schools, summer workshops, correspondence and authentic conversation. Among the many, I must mention my gratitude to Rebecca L. Jordan, Roma Hammel, Doris Dillon, Elaine V. Howes, Susan Hall, Don Hill, Sally McClintock, Jacquie Killingsworth and Kim Anderson. Of course, the limitations of this book reflect my own shortcomings, not those of my friends and colleagues.

I am indebted to the editors of the following journals and the publishers of the following edited volumes for allowing me to publish in slightly modified forms several parts of this book: Christopher M. Clark (1993), The good teacher, reprinted from *English Teachers' Journal* (Israel), **46** (May), 29–34; published by The English Inspectorate, Ministry of Education and Culture, Jerusalem and reprinted by permission of the publisher; Christopher M. Clark (1985), Research into practice: cautions and qualifications. In T. Raphael (ed.), *The Contexts of School-Based Literacy*; published by Random House, Inc. and reprinted with permission of the publisher (here entitled 'Research in the Service of Teaching'); Christopher M. Clark (1990), Real lessons from imaginary teachers, *Journal of Curriculum Studies*, **23**, (5), 429–433; published by Taylor & Francis Ltd. and reprinted with permission of the publisher; Christopher M. Clark (1990), The teacher and the taught. In J. I. Goodlad, R. Soder and K. A. Sirotnik (eds), *The Moral Dimensions of Teaching*; published by Jossey-Bass Inc. and reprinted with permission of the publisher (here titled 'Case One: Teaching William a Lesson,' 'Case Two: The Gatekeeper's Dilemma,' 'Case Three: No Respect for Carlos,' and 'Reflections on Three Cases'); Christopher M. Clark (1990), 'What you can learn from applesauce'. In E. Eisner and A. Peshkin (eds), *Qualitative Inquiry in Education: The Continuing Debate*; published by Teachers' College, Columbia University, and reprinted with permission of the publisher; Christopher M. Clark (1988), Asking the right questions about teacher preparation: contributions from research on teacher thinking, *Educational Researcher*, **17**, (2), 5–12; published by the American Educational Research Association and reprinted by permission of the publisher; Christopher M. Clark (1992), Teachers as designers in self-directed professional development. In A. Hargreaves and M. G. Fullan (eds), *Understanding Teacher Development*; published by Teachers' College, Columbia University, and reprinted by permission of the publisher. I am also grateful for permission to reproduce the haiku poem by Irene (p. 51). In E. S. Richardson (1964) *In the Early World*; published by the New Zealand Council of Educational Research.

Introduction

Teaching is like a story, like a journey. Story and journey are familiar patterns with infinite variations. Each story and each journey is special, distinct from all others. Yet all stories share some common features, as do journeys. I expect that you are well into your own story and journey of teaching, whether this is your 10th day in a teacher education programme or your 10,000th as a teacher of children or adults. If so, this book is for you. Think of *Thoughtful Teaching* as a companion on your unfolding journey and as food for thought as you plan, live, retell and involve others in your story.

WHAT IS THOUGHTFUL TEACHING?

With the words 'thoughtful teaching' I want to highlight two important aspects of the lives and work of teachers. The first is that teaching is an intellectual enterprise. Teachers are representatives of academic disciplines who must themselves work to understand the knowledge, traditions, and terminology of mathematics, science, history, language and the arts, and continually deal with the intellectual challenge of representing knowledge usefully and understandably to their students. Teaching demands a great deal of thought, in the classic forms of study, problem solving, and decision-making.

The second sense of 'thoughtful' is closer to our everyday use of the word. When I hear a person described as thoughtful, I understand this to mean considerate of another, particularly of the feelings of another. A thoughtful person is empathic. He or she knows how I feel and responds to me in ways that comfort, reassure and encourage. A thoughtful person is able to do two things well: see and feel life from the perspective of another, and say and do the right things when we most need that help and support. In contrast, we say that a person has been 'thoughtless' when he or she acts insensitively or hurtfully towards others, even when their actions are logical and justifiable on intellectual grounds.

Teaching can never be completely thoughtless in the first sense of the term. If you teach, you must think at some level about what you are teaching, how you are teaching, and who you are teaching. Teaching is inescapably intellectual.

And a considerable body of research has grown up to describe the career-long intellectual journey. Teachers' minds are much less a mystery than they were a generation ago.

But thoughtful teaching as being genuinely considerate of children and colleagues is less well documented and possibly less common. Biographical and autobiographical accounts of school life describe painfully insensitive teaching. Too often the intellectual mission of schooling is cast in opposition to the social and personal dimensions of life in classrooms: excellence vs. equity; rigorous standards vs. social promotion; tough mindedness against tender heartedness; competition vs. cooperation; rational–scientific over intuitive–personal ways of knowing. Being a thoughtful teacher in this second sense often requires teaching against the grain.

In calling for more thoughtful teaching I hope to encourage teachers and teacher-educators to develop in both meanings of the term. The intellectual and the relational aspects of teaching are both vital, from preschool to graduate school, and everywhere in between. When teachers encounter dilemmas that pit head against heart, or distant authority against local wisdom, life gets more complicated and more interesting.

ORGANIZATION

This book is divided into four parts. Part One, Reflections on Thoughtful Teaching, lays out the terrain in broad strokes, making a case for the importance of teachers to the quality of education, showing how researchers of different persuasions, teachers, and children understand good teaching, and arguing that the moral dimension of teaching is as important as the cognitive.

Part Two, Research and Thoughtful Teaching, offers a perspective on thinking critically and creatively about educational research and what it does and does not promise to practising teachers.

Part Three, Portraits of Thoughtful Teaching, consists of five case descriptions of episodes that called for thoughtfulness, courage, and common sense in real school situations.

Part Four, Cultivating Thoughtful Teaching, suggests how teachers and teacher-educators can encourage and sustain themselves and the next generation in the essential work of thoughtful teaching.

CAVEAT EMPTOR

May I tell you what this book is not? *Thoughtful Teaching* is not a manual of answers, prescriptions, or tricks of the trade. Many books and workshops promise all the answers to foolproof teaching. But few teachers are fools. *Thoughtful Teaching* is not an exhaustive catalogue of scientifically distilled results of research on teaching, curriculum, or child learning and development. After reviewing and doing considerable research in education, I have found that only bits and snippets have been of direct and practical help to teachers at the chalkface. I have referred to one hundred or so research studies and scholarly books and journal articles throughout the text. But I have done this more to locate my point of view in the conversations among researchers and teachers than to justify my claims or to create an exhaustive bibliography.

Finally, *Thoughtful Teaching* is not a call to drop your story, your journey, and substitute my script. I sincerely hope that the information, perspectives, and inspiration you may take away from reading this book and from conversations about the ideas you encounter herein serve you well. But in the end, as at the beginning, you are the author, lead actor, and most critical audience of your tale.

NOTE

Although this book has been written from an American perspective, all situations and conclusions are applicable to all teachers. I have used a commonly understood term when able, and otherwise have indicated in parentheses an equivalent term.

PART ONE

REFLECTIONS ON THOUGHTFUL TEACHING

Chapter 1

Teachers and the Quality of Education

As teaching goes, so goes the nation. Schooling is organized so that educational policies, curriculum, and instruction are interpreted and enacted by teachers. Teachers are the human point of contact with students. All other influences on the quality of education are mediated by who the teacher is and what the teacher does. Teachers have the potential for enhancing the quality of education by bringing life to curriculum and inspiring students to curiosity and self-directed learning. And teachers can also degrade the quality of education through error, laziness, cruelty or incompetence. For better or for worse, teachers determine the quality of education.

A common reason given for deciding to become a teacher is 'I just love kids'. This is a good reason, a worthy motive for beginning the journey towards thoughtful teaching. The ultimate purpose of teaching is to serve children on their own journeys to adulthood, citizenship and leadership of the next generation. In a sense, the future quality of civilized society depends on the good work of teachers today. This may seem like a heavy responsibility for ordinary teachers to bear. But naming the teacher's burden does not make it more or less real. The 15,000 hours children spend in the company of teachers is inevitably formative. 'I touch the future – I teach' captures the idea in six words.

Admittedly, there is more to teaching than feeling affection for children. Yet without love and eagerness to serve schoolchildren well, teaching loses its heart. And when teachers forget that children come first, their students and society are in serious danger.

What does it mean for teachers to believe that children come first? It means that schooling is, at its roots, a matter of human relationships. The web of relationships in a kindergarten or a secondary school is complex and dynamic, reaching beyond the classroom walls to include parents, siblings, janitors, school secretaries, the principal (headteacher), sports coaches, and many others. The classroom teacher is at the centre of this network, very influential in setting the relational tone. Will we be cooperative or competitive, generous or stingy, preoccupied with enforcing rules or with flexibility, compassion and common sense? Will this set of relationships be optimistic or pessimistic, full of possibility or of subtle disapproval and outright punishment? 'Children come first' means that thoughtful teachers ask questions like these again and again as they fine-tune the tone of their relationships with children, individually and collectively.

There are no simple recipes or techniques to guarantee that the relational tone of a classroom will always be positive and constructive. Cooperative learning groups, for example, can be played out in a huge variety of positive or socially divisive ways. And, influential as he or she is, one teacher cannot dictate the morale of the whole community. Conflicts large and small and dilemmas that would tax the wisdom of Solomon surface at the most inconvenient times in the life of a healthy school. What is essential is to remember, to remind oneself, that the ultimate point of schooling is not technical, or legal, or political, or even academic, but relational. Asking 'What can I do here today to encourage, to nurture, to improve the quality of life?' is the vital first principle of thoughtful teaching.

ROLES OF THE TEACHER

There are three roles of the teacher that most directly influence the quality of education: teacher as person, teacher as curriculum planner and teacher as instructor. As a person, a teacher is changing and developing, advancing and regressing, experiencing the joys and disappointments of life just as all adults do. At the same time, a teacher is a powerful adult in a world of children. For most schoolchildren, their teacher is the adult with whom they have the greatest amount of daily contact. Teachers therefore have significant opportunities to influence the personal development of their impressionable students. Teachers act as potential role models of responsible adult behaviour, attitudes and values. And the teacher is the architect of the social system of the classroom, with its rules, norms, sanctions and rewards. The social system of the classroom sets the tone and context for human interaction for an entire school year. And the personality and values of the teacher are clearly reflected in how life in a classroom is lived out. Parents of schoolchildren know that who the teacher is as a person has a profound effect on the quality of education that their children experience.

As curriculum planners, teachers call the tune to which they and their students dance and sing. Sometimes a teacher is responsible for creating his or her own curriculum. Then the quality of education's content depends most directly on the teacher. In these situations, the teacher (or perhaps a small group of teachers) judges the worthiness of what shall be learned, and also creates the materials, activities, and approaches most likely to achieve these learning goals. The positive side of this situation is that the teacher who creates curriculum will have studied the content thoroughly, knows the relationships among parts of the curriculum, and has feelings of ownership and enthusiasm about it. The negative side is that many teachers do not have the subject matter expertise, planning expertise or the time to write worthwhile, accurate, practical and attractive curricula.

But even when the teacher is not responsible for literally creating curriculum, the quality of education is affected by his or her interpretation of it. Through planning and decision-making teachers inevitably change the curriculum from exactly what was intended by the authors to that which is actually experienced in the classroom. These transformations of the curriculum into action involve the content, pace and emphasis of instruction. By adapting the curriculum as published to fit the special circumstances of one's own subject matter knowledge, beliefs, priorities, and unique classroom situation, the quality of education is changed. Sometimes these changes bring improvements; at other times they degrade the quality of education. But teachers' transformations of curriculum seem to be necessary responses to the complexity, unpredictability, and uniqueness of each classroom situation. The teacher, one way or another, determines what is taught.

The third path of influence on the quality of education is through instruction, the image that we think of first when we hear the word 'teaching'. Here we are primarily concerned with how teachers speak and act in the presence of students with the intention of changing what they know, understand and can do. Student change is at the centre of the agenda for the instructor and, in the best of circumstances, for the students as well. Lecturing, demonstration, discussion leading, storytelling, practice with feedback, recitation, and organizing simulations are just a few of the forms that instruction takes. One of the marks of the veteran master teacher is that he or she has a repertoire of different forms of instruction that can be called up at will, mixed and matched to fit the demands and opportunities of the moment. The beginning teacher, in contrast, may be naturally drawn to one form of instruction, but be uncomfortable or barely competent with others. It is typical, for example, for prospective secondary school teachers to resolve, 'I shall never lecture to my students. Lectures are boring'. No doubt we have all been subjected to far too many boring lectures. But boredom is a side effect of a badly organized or poorly delivered lecture, or of one that is mismatched to the background knowledge and expectations of the audience. So the task of the beginner, and to some extent of all developing teachers, is to extend, analyse, and practise the full palette of instructional forms.

Most of us have probably been taught by at least one teacher who can be described as a person who really knows the content well but cannot get it across to students. This kind of teacher is one whose deficiencies in using instructional or management skills compromise the quality of education. Or, on the positive side, you can probably remember teachers who were inspiring lecturers, or brilliant leaders of Socratic discussions, or the perfect model of organization and order. These are the people we look to for inspiration in the profession and whom we try to enlist as mentors to student teachers and beginners. These are the kinds of teaching we hope our best teacher education programs will foster and our strongest programmes of professional development will continue to support.

How teachers behave during instruction is surely a major influence on the quality of education.

To summarize, teachers influence the quality of education in both positive and negative ways. These influences take place through three roles that all teachers enact: teacher as person, as curriculum planner, and as instructor. Weakness in any one of these three domains can degrade the quality of education. Strength in all three is the goal of teacher education and of continuing professional development. 'Thoughtful teaching' is my way of describing the career-long search for excellence in and balance among these three pillars supporting the edifice of quality education.

Chapter 2

The Good Teacher

This is the story of the search for the good teacher. It draws on three sources: 1) research on teaching, 2) the voices of teachers themselves and 3) what children say about good teaching. My own memories of experiences as a student, teacher and parent of school children are also represented here. I intend that these words will create a composite picture of the good teacher in your mind – an idealized image, like Leonardo's Mona Lisa – that inspires but may not be imitated unreflectively. Or like Michelangelo's David – a heroic form on which we can project our own best qualities and aspirations, magnified in excellent proportion, larger than life and radically encouraging to the human spirit.

Knowing something of the good teacher will not, by itself, solve the many problems of education, professional development, and life-long learning about which we are all concerned. But coming to a better vision of good teaching may serve to encourage each of us as we address specific personal, local and national problems in our own creative and sensitive ways. For, in the final analysis, the good teacher equips his or her students for confident, independent thought and action in an uncertain world. The good teacher prepares children for a world of difference. The good teacher knows when to let us go. And this is almost always before we feel ready to be on our own.

Before summarizing what researchers on teaching have to say about the good teacher, I want to tell a story of teaching, learning and leadership. The story is of a man who was captain of a submarine in which I served as chief engineer. Captain Carlin is 12 years older than I am. We were born and schooled in the same neighbourhood of the city of Philadelphia. As captain of the submarine, he was a man of good humour, profound competence, and high expectations for his officers and men. He was a good teacher.

A submarine is a complex and intense place to live and learn. The three different submarines in which I served were, basically, steel cylinders 16 feet in diameter and 300 feet long, crammed with all manner of equipment and people. It is an extremely intense learning environment. The safety of the 75 crew members depends, to a great extent, on how well everyone learns to operate and repair every electrical, hydraulic, electronic, mechanical and pneumatic system on board. Everyone has a personal interest in everyone else's learning. Our lives depend on the competence of the newest crew member. This makes for a highly motivated learning community.

In this exotic context, what made Captain Carlin a good teacher? In part, it was his affirmative personality, good humour, and encouragement by example. He was very competent and knowledgeable about all aspects of submarine operations, and he was also open to learning new ways of doing things. He was eager for deeper understandings of the ship, the sea, and of the people with whom he worked and lived. He recognized that the unique character of this particular submarine must be learned patiently over time. He also taught me that the character of the crew could be cultivated but not imposed from above. He knew that building on the strengths of each individual crew member is crucial, and that expressing respect for and interest in each person was one of the keys to his leadership. In part, he managed by wandering around the submarine, collecting each of our stories.

But lest you think that Captain Carlin was larger than life, he also showed us his human frailties and vulnerabilities. He did all of the grocery shopping for his family of six. He mowed his own lawn. He was uncertain about how to raise his four children, and, as a father of pre-adolescents at the end of the 1960s, he had many reasonable fears about what could befall his boys and girls. He had car trouble, and he chewed his fingernails. He not only collected stories from each of us, he also told stories of his own life, his childhood, his weekend, and of his chilling feelings when he was missile officer on a Polaris submarine during the Cuban missile crisis.

One other fact about Captain Carlin will help you appreciate him as a leader and a teacher: he put great energy into promoting and publishing the accomplishments of our ship and crew to the Division Commander and to the Squadron Commander. Our captain was our advocate; he was the teller of good news, the one who made us proud to be on the USS Amberjack. We rose to the occasion; we fed his need to tell good news by creating more of it. Both years during which he was our captain, we were awarded the highest honours for operational readiness.

One morning we were returning from two weeks at sea, and I was to be the Officer of the Deck, to bring the ship upriver and moor alongside the pier. Shiphandling in this situation is a difficult and hazardous team effort, and I was a relatively inexperienced 25-year- old shiphandler. The captain stood behind me on the open bridge as I navigated the river, came through a narrow drawbridge, and gave orders to helm and engine room that brought us smoothly alongside the pier. It was a very good landing.

What was the captain's role in this good landing? First, he kept silent throughout, letting me know that I was in charge. Second, he was present and alert, giving me the reassurance that, if the situation became especially difficult, I could call on him for help. And third, he was sufficiently aware of the particulars of solving this complex piloting problem, on this particular day, that his congratulations to me and our debriefing afterwards carried great meaning, credibility and instructional value. I still remember his first words of that conversation of 25 years ago. The captain said, 'Lieutenant Clark, that was a fine landing. It cost me only three fingernails.'

So here we have the beginnings of a portrait of the good teacher, in a setting quite different from school. Please bear these qualities of Captain Carlin in mind as we shift attention to what researchers on teaching have to say about the good teacher.

WHAT DO RESEARCHERS SAY?

The question 'What makes a good teacher?' is fundamental to much of research in education. This is particularly true for three approaches to research on teaching conceived and led by educational psychologists: The Process–Product approach, the Teacher Thinking approach, and the Teacher Knowledge approach. Let us now see what each of these research traditions tells us about good teaching.

1. Process–Product Research on Teaching

The Process–Product approach to research on teaching began in the USA in the early 1950s. The young educational psychologists of that time were fresh from designing emergency training programmes for soldiers, sailors and airmen in World War II. Naturally, they drew on their experiences and successes with task analysis, behaviour reinforcement, and testing and measurement when they turned their attention to teachers and schooling. Their goals were to discover the secrets of success of the most effective teachers and then to create teacher training programmes that could transform all teachers into very effective ones.

The reason this approach is called the Process–Product approach is that the researchers concerned themselves with two classes of variables. 'Process' refers to the visible and audible behaviour of teachers and students during classroom teaching. 'Product' refers to the objectively measurable results of teaching, usually expressed as achievement test scores of children. The good teacher, in this framework, is one whose students achieve the highest scores on tests of knowledge and skill, following instruction. The research programme is dedicated to describing the teaching skills and behaviours that reliably distinguish between the most effective teachers and their less effective counterparts.

Forty years of Process–Product research on teaching generated many developments in the tools used to study teaching. Observation systems for describing teacher behaviour and classroom interaction have become progressively more sophisticated and complex. Use of technology such as audio-recording, videotape, and direct computer coding of data make possible complex studies that could not have been attempted 15 or 20 years ago. And the technologies of testing and data analysis have also become more powerful and precise during our lifetime. Most importantly, thousands of researchers have spent tens of thousands of hours in school classrooms, carefully attending to teachers and teaching, students and learning. A scholarly community of research on teaching has developed internationally; a community of dedicated and intelligent professionals that has come to some concensus about what makes a good teacher. What do these people tell us today about the good teacher?

To answer this question I will draw on the extensive literature review by Brophy and Good, 'Teacher Behavior and Student Achievement', published in the third edition of the *Handbook of Research on Teaching* (Wittrock, 1986). Their summary and integration of the findings of Process–Product research emphasizes results of studies that have been replicated a number of times and in which these reviewers have particularly high confidence. According to Brophy and Good, the most reliable findings about effective teaching depict a classroom teacher who is well organized, efficient, task-oriented and businesslike. They describe this form of active, direct instruction as follows:

> Students achieve more in classes where they spend most of their time being taught or supervised by their teachers rather than working on their own (or not working at all). These classes include frequent lessons ... in which the teacher presents information and develops concepts through lecture and demonstration, elaborates this information in the feedback given following responses to recitation or discussion questions, prepares the students for follow up seatwork activities by giving instructions and going through practice examples, monitors progress on assignments after releasing the students to work independently, and follows up with appropriate feedback and reteaching when necessary. The teacher carries the content to the students personally rather than depending on the curriculum materials to do so, but conveys information mostly in brief presentations followed by recitation or application opportunities. There is a great deal of teacher talk, but most of it is academic rather than procedural or managerial, and much of it involves asking questions and giving feedback rather than extended lecturing (p. 361).

So, the image of the good teacher offered by Process–Product researchers is one where the teacher is the efficient director and manager of a three-part instructional process that involves lecture and demonstration, recitation with feedback, and supervised practice or seatwork. This body of research also offers guidance in considerable detail about which behaviours constitute effective recitation, or feedback, or appropriate seatwork. For example, the researchers have analysed the recitation strategy of teaching into a three-part pattern consisting of structuring information, question asking and responding to student answers. Breaking the strategy down even further, many studies have been done to discover what kinds of questions at what levels of difficulty are correlated with high student achievement. Similar studies have also been done of the varieties of structured information giving, of responding to students' correct or incorrect answers, of the pacing of instruction, of grouping for instruction, and of managing seatwork and homework assignments.

The global image of the good teacher supported by this research is of a businesslike person who is clearly in control of the flow of work in an orderly, efficient classroom. Such a person is clear, well organized, enthusiastic and direct. The process of rapid and progressive coverage of academic content, with clear feedback and remedial instruction when necessary, leads to superior performance on tests of facts and skills. The culture of control, efficiency and objective measurement of learning outcomes defines the world of the Process–Product teacher.

2. Research on Teacher Thinking

Partly as a reaction to the behavioural and managerial focus of Process–Product research on teaching, a new approach to the question 'Who is the good teacher?' began in 1975. This approach is called Research on Teacher Thinking, and concerns itself with the mental lives of teachers – the planning, decision-making, beliefs and theories that invisibly guide and influence teacher action. This field began with the image of a teacher as a diagnostician: observing, categorizing and acting in response to a complex array of cues and situations that described self, students and learning environment. The metaphor of teacher as decision-maker became central to this work, along with the assumption that teachers behave rationally almost all of the time. The challenge to researchers was to describe and understand the rationality underlying good teaching.

In a review summarizing approximately 40 studies of Teacher Thinking my colleague Penelope Peterson and I conclude with this portrait of the good teacher:

> First, the research shows that thinking plays an important part in teaching, and that the image of a teacher as a reflective professional ... is not far fetched. Teachers do plan in a rich variety of ways, and these plans have real consequences in the classroom. Teachers do have thoughts and make decisions frequently ... during interactive teaching. Teachers do have theories and belief systems that influence their perceptions, plans and actions. This literature has given us an opportunity to broaden our appreciation for what teaching is by adding rich descriptions of the mental activities of teachers to the existing body of work that describes the visible behavior of teachers.
>
> The emerging picture of the teacher as a reflective professional is a developmental one that begins during undergraduate teacher

education . . . and continues to grow and change with professional experience. The education majors who would become professionals in this sense are firmly grounded in the disciplines and subject matters that they will teach. Their study of subject matter focuses on both content and on the cognitive organization of that content in ways useful to themselves and their future students. They have had both supervised practice in using the behavioral skills and strategies of teaching and have also been initiated into the less visible aspects of teaching, including the full variety of types of planning and interactive decision making. The maturing professional teacher is one who has taken some steps toward making explicit his or her implicit theories and beliefs about learners, curriculum, subject matter, and the teacher's role. This teacher has developed a style of planning for instruction that includes several interrelated types of planning and that has become more streamlined and automatic with experience. Much of this teacher's interactive teaching consists of routines familiar to the students, thus decreasing the collective information-processing load. During teaching, the teacher attends to and intently processes academic and nonacademic . . . events and cues. These experienced teachers have developed the confidence to depart from a planned course of action when they judge that to be appropriate. They reflect on and analyze the apparent effects of their own teaching and apply the results of these reflections to their future plans and actions. In short, they have become researchers on their own teaching effectiveness (Clark and Peterson, 1986, pp. 292–3).

We leave research on Teacher Thinking with the impression that the good teacher's effective action depends as much on thoughts, plans and decisions as on efficient behaviour and management ability. The mental lives of teachers are at least as important to understanding and supporting the profession as are their visible behaviours.

3. Research on Teacher Knowledge

One of the newest approaches to research on teaching is called Research on Teacher Knowledge, and its practitioners take the position that what is most important and most neglected in teaching is the teacher's knowledge of the subject matter that he or she teaches. Logic and common sense suggest that one cannot teach well what one does not understand. But how many of us have had the experience of being taught by a teacher or professor who is clearly expert at a discipline, but who is unable to communicate that knowledge to struggling students? This odd yet commonplace problem has led Shulman and his colleagues at Stanford University to initiate a series of case studies of the knowledge held by high school teachers and, most importantly, of the ways in which these teachers transform that knowledge in order to represent it to their students.

What these detailed case studies depict, in the teaching of history, of science, of literature, and of mathematics is what Claude Levi-Strauss calls a 'conversation with the situation' (Levi-Strauss, 1967). This conversation takes place in the mind of the teacher as he or she reorganizes academic knowledge about Shakespeare's *Hamlet* or the process of photosynthesis to accommodate to local knowledge about the lives and minds of the children to be taught. A delicate balance must be struck each day between appropriate transformation of knowledge and the danger of distorting that which is to be taught. In this framework, the teacher is both a knowledgable representative of an academic discipline and also a translator who can faithfully express the big ideas of history or biology in the language of 16-year-olds.

This would be a difficult enough task if all 16-year-olds spoke the same language. But according to these researchers, the teacher is faced with many dialects and variations in students' ways of understanding. One of the best known scholarly reports of this research effort is '150 Different Ways of Knowing' (Wilson, Shulman and Richert, 1987). This title is intended to emphasize the fact that a secondary school teacher who teaches 150 students each day ought to aspire to a repertoire of many variations in ways to represent content to the many different 'ways of knowing' personified by those students.

L. S. Shulman, in 'Knowledge and teaching: foundations of the new reform' (1987) describes the philosophy and assumptions of research on teacher knowledge. Shulman (1987) lists seven constituents of teacher knowledge:

- content knowledge;
- general pedagogical knowledge;
- curriculum knowledge;
- pedagogical content knowledge;
- knowledge of learners and their characteristics;
- knowledge of educational contexts;
- knowledge of educational ends, purposes, and values (p. 8).

In my opinion, the central contributions of this approach to research on teaching are the coining of the concept of *pedagogical content knowledge* and the descriptions of particular cases of teachers developing and acting on this 'special amalgam of content and pedagogy that is the unique province of teachers' (Shulman, 1987, p. 8). Good teachers, then, must not only know how to manage, give feedback, make practical plans and wise decisions. They must be more than performers, more than thinkers. The good teacher must also be a practical scholar, a student of the academic disciplines, and a fluent translator. The good

13

teacher becomes a life-long learner of subject matter and of ways to represent it.

WHAT DO TEACHERS SAY?

So, now we have a picture of the good teacher from the points of view of the educational research community. You probably know teachers who fit these descriptions. You or your children may have been taught by teachers who exhibit these qualities. You may know yourself to be a good teacher in these ways. But is it good enough to demonstrate comprehensive mastery of subject matter, to exhibit technical skills in managing a classroom and explaining its complexities, and to be an effective planner and decision-maker? Is it good enough to score high on teacher evaluation checklists developed from research on teaching?

For some answers to these questions, listen to what teachers have said about what it takes to be a good teacher, to what good teachers have said about themselves, and to what ordinary teachers have said about times when their teaching was exceptionally good. These answers come from my conversations with and interviews of 60 American secondary and primary school teachers.

The teachers who have spoken to me about good teaching agree with much of the advice we have heard from researchers on teaching. In fact, experienced teachers often react to reports of research by saying 'Of course! Everyone knows that. Why did you need to do an expensive study to demonstrate what is obvious?' Yet mixed with this somewhat sceptical attitude towards research is an element of gratitude and appreciation for the thoughtful attention and support that research on teaching has brought to an underappreciated and isolated profession.

What is different about the teachers' voice in the conversation about good teaching is what is in the foreground. To teachers, the heart of good teaching is not in management or decision-making or pedagogical content knowledge. No, the essence of good teaching, for teachers, is in the arena of human relationships. Teaching is good when a class becomes a community of honest, nurturant and mutually respectful people. Experienced teachers treasure the moments and memories of times when laughter, compassion and surprise described their day or year. Cultivation of the self esteem of young people is very high on the list of goals of the good teacher. Better to leave my class having learned a little mathematics and love it than knowing a lot of mathematics and hate it. This is a case where the common sense of good teachers is supported by fascinating research: in one of a series of studies of the phenomenon of 'flow' by University of Chicago psychologists, the research team found that, independent of student ability, their performance was best in classes they saw as 'enjoyable' (Csikszentmihalyi and Larson, 1984).

Good humour was mentioned again and again as a quality of the best teachers remembered. Enthusiasm for teaching, fascination with the content, and openness to admitting mistakes are important in good teachers. The good teacher is capable of expressing love, care and respect in 150 different ways. The good teacher is an adult who takes children seriously. The good teacher, they say, is the colleague who supports me and is open to my support.

As I listened to experienced educators speak of the good teacher, the word 'good' took on richer meaning. The good teacher became one who could find that which is good in his or her students, individually and collectively. The pedagogical challenge becomes one of how to celebrate and elaborate the noblest human qualities in the context of a school. For teaching is a social and a moral enterprise. Teaching is more than the transmission of information. Intentionally or not, teachers shape the character of their students and influence the character of society for years after they retire. The good teacher attends to this human, social, moral dimension of life in schools as much as to the technical and academic. Good teaching is a vocation, a calling, as much as it is a profession.

WHAT DO CHILDREN SAY?

The last voice that we shall hear speak about the good teacher is, perhaps, the most important: the voice of children. What do the children say? I have listened to little children, to adolescents and to adult students. I urge you to listen for the voice of your own childhood memories; to imagine or remember what you and your own children know to be true about good teaching. Almost invariably, children's thoughts and stories about good teachers concern four fundamental human needs: 1) to be known, 2) to be encouraged, 3) to be respected and 4) to be led. (These four human needs are the positive side of four primal fears that children and adults labour against throughout life: fear of abandonment, of despair, of ridicule, and of being lost.)

In the language of children, their good teachers nurture them by treating them as intelligent people who can become even more intelligent, by taking the time to learn who we are and what we love, treating us fairly by treating us differently, by explaining why he teaches and acts as he does, by telling stories of her own life outside school and listening to ours, by letting me have a bad day when I can't help it. The good teacher is both funny and serious. We can laugh together, and this makes me feel happy and close. She puts thought into surprising us in ways that we will never forget. He draws pictures that show how ideas are connected; we don't feel lost or afraid that we will be sent away or humiliated. The good teacher loves what he is teaching, but does not show off or put distance between us. The good teacher sets things up so that children can learn how to learn from one another. She knows how to be a friend while still a responsible adult.

Very often, the good teacher does not know of the good he has done at the time. A letter to a teacher written five years after graduation from university closes with these words:

> You were a good friend when I needed one. You listened to me
> ramble on. You said encouraging things at the right times. When I
> was a confused student you made time for me. There were times
> when I was ready to burst that I came and took comfort from your
> confidence and your soothing voice.

The good teacher puts people first, say the children. The good teacher acts from love and caring, and is loved and cared for in return.

SUMMING UP

Now we have heard from researchers, from teachers, and from children about the good teacher. The composite picture may seem overwhelming – too much for any human being to become, too much for any teacher training programme or national plan to guarantee. Yet I am optimistic, for the voices that speak of the good teacher describe real people, actual classrooms, true stories, powerful experiences. This is not wishful thinking, fantasy, or groundless idealization. These are authentic voices of inspiration and encouragement. One secondary schoolgirl with whom I spoke estimated that about one-third of the 30 teachers she had been taught by were good teachers in these ways.

Perhaps it is now time to change the question. Let us turn away from asking 'Who is the good teacher?' Instead, let us ask 'When is teaching good?' How can we each do a better job of acknowledging the good teaching that is already happening every day in our schools? How can we improve policy, conditions, and support systems so that teachers can have good moments and good days more often? We should begin to build an ethos of good teaching by learning to tell stories, even sagas, of heroic but invisible good teaching. We need help from minstrels, poets, biographers, historians, and film producers to create a vivid literature of good teaching. We need help from clinical psychologists and from one another to heal our childhood wounds and prevent us from unthinkingly passing them on to the next generation. As teachers, we need to learn to respect the children by learning to respect and love the wounded child within each of us. To cultivate good teaching we must begin with ourselves.

Good teaching will never be easy. Nor will it ever by easy to be a good parent, a good nurse, a good scientist, or a good political leader. The essence of these callings is a courageous willingness to form moral relationships, to embrace uncertainty, to do what seems right at the time, to lead but not to control. In these ways, good teaching happens every day in our schools and in our homes, in our workplaces and towns. Perhaps the best preparation for the future of life-long learning, in this culture and elsewhere, is to cultivate and treasure a better appreciation of the present state of good teaching. We cannot change the past, but we can come to understand and cooperate with contemporary goodness more constructively.

CONCLUSION

I would like to close these reflections on the search for the good teacher by quoting part of a letter to a master teacher. She is an outstanding teacher of little children, and she wrote asking advice and support in her new role as mentor to new teachers. I did send her some scholarly papers on teacher education and professional development, but I think that my best advice and encouragement came from these words:

> The most important contributions you can make to the growth of new teachers come from things that you already know. Your alertness, empathy, intuition and resourcefulness in doing exciting things with simple materials and opportunities – this is a rich lode to mine on behalf of students and young teachers. Your sense of the pace and rhythm of the school year and of child development in all of its unevenness is what children and new teachers need to see and hear and sense from you. The courage to go forward in the face of uncertainty comes from your trust, hope, and willingness to take risks. You know, too, that almost no teaching disaster is too disastrous to fix up, start over, or to do better next week. Teaching is difficult, risky business, but you know that it helps your students when you make the easiness and joy shine through.
>
> Finally, and most fundamentally, you respect each of your students. Each is different from you, but worthwhile and needing to be taken seriously by you. Your respect for them and your openness to learn from them makes teaching a relationship rather than a contest of wills.
>
> These, I think, are the qualities that you personify as a good teacher. This is the well from which you can draw again and again to refresh yourself, your students, and your friends.

Now, like Captain Carlin, I am alert yet silent, eager to support you in your efforts to promote and celebrate good and thoughtful teaching. I wish you great success, and look forward to your stories. So far, this has cost me only three fingernails.

EPILOGUE

Six months after I wrote this paper I sent a copy to Captain Carlin's address in Alexandria, Virginia. We had been out of contact for six or seven years. I included a note to the effect that I hoped he didn't mind being used as an example of a good teacher when he was merely trying to be a good sailor. Two weeks later I received a letter from Barbara Carlin, Bob's wife, which said, in part:

Bob died on October 25, 1988. He had interstitial fibrosis, a lung disease for which there is no known cause or cure. The children and I were so touched by your remembrances of Bob. He would have been pleased and proud, and probably would have said: 'I wasn't quite *that* good.' Thank you for a beautiful tribute to Bob and to all good teachers. You have touched our hearts.

Chapter 3

The Moral Dimension of Teaching

In Great Britain, in America, all over Europe, from Canada to Australia, two voices are heard about the nature of teaching. The first, and louder voice, says that teaching is a profession, and, as such, should share both the privileges and the responsibilities of other professions, notably medicine and law. Researchers on teaching, and particularly researchers on the psychology of teaching, have first assumed that teaching should be profitably thought of as a high status design profession. Since 1976 researchers have proceeded to study psychological aspects of teachers that are conspicuous in the work of physicians, architects, lawyers, and military strategists: mental processes such as diagnostic skill, planning, decision-making, problem solving, reflection, and theorizing. Not surprisingly, they have found some support for what they set out to discover. Examined in a certain light, with particular research techniques, we can see a family resemblance between the thoughts of teachers and the thinking of other professionals.

The second voice raised about the nature of teaching sings an old song: that teaching is a fundamentally moral craft (Tom, 1984; Sockett, 1993). Those who call our attention to the moral dimensions of teaching tend to be philosophers rather than psychologists. Their arguments, case studies, and rhetoric often have as much to say against the image of teaching being primarily a technical-rational activity as they do about what it means for teaching to be understood as a fundamentally moral pursuit. Yet this line of scholarship has had considerable success in persuading educationalists, teacher-educators, and practising teachers that the work of teachers is profoundly moral, in its day-to-day actions and in its consequences.

Through my own research on teaching thinking, and through my more recent thinking and writing on the moral dimensions of teaching, I have made modest contributions to both of these schools of thought. I have held up the image of 'teacher as reflective professional' as the end to be desired of any thoughtful programme of professional development. I have joined the chorus of those who urge veteran teachers to become 'researchers on their own teaching'. And I have written about cases in which the conscious and unconscious acts of teachers have had important moral consequences, for better and for worse, in the lives of their students. Spending time in schools, in regular contact with teachers and children, and thinking about my hopes and fears as a parent of schoolchildren have persuaded me that the ethical intuition of a good teacher is frequently as important as her mathematical sophistication or his pedagogical skill.

For teachers and for teacher-educators these two voices, these two lines of research, pose some difficult practical problems. In theory, research on teaching is offered as illuminating description of the best of the status quo – a source of insight and long overdue appreciation for the complexity of teachers' everyday work. But in practice, research on teaching usually is linked to efforts to change, to improve, to repair, to reform teachers and their ways. To describe excellent teaching is, at the same time, to set a goal, a standard against which to judge excellence. It is but a short step from appreciation of the few to evaluation of the many. Description becomes prescription, often with less and less regard for the contextual matters that make the description meaningful in the first place. A certain bounded understanding of teaching by a few researchers can become the duty of all teachers.

MESSAGES FROM RESEARCHERS

To sum up the messages from the research communities, researchers on teacher thinking say: 'Be very thoughtful, reflective, self-conscious, and intentional all of the time. This is the secret of good teaching.' Those who theorize and write about the moral dimension of teaching say: 'Be good all of the time. And be especially aware of the ethical and moral implications of everything you do, for the future of the human race depends on your good effects on children.' These are very strong messages; very heavy responsibilities with which to charge teachers; and, by extension, very heavy responsibilities for supervisors, evaluators and the teachers of teachers. These cognitive and moral imperatives often conflict – what may be effective instruction for some, say, teaching maths at the learning pace of the most gifted students in a class, may at the same time be morally questionable for those left gasping in the dust. Sometimes doing what the heart tells us is right moves us away from what the curriculum guide calls for us to teach. These are dilemmas across domains, that go beyond the well-documented dilemmas with which teachers struggle in both instruction and moral action (Lampert, 1985; Ball and Wilson, 1993).

I shall not dwell on the ways in which teachers' work is complicated and enabled by the implications and prescriptions of psychological research on teaching. Cognitive science, as it has been applied to the study of teaching, draws heavily on studies of the psychology of decision-making and problem solving in well-defined problem situations, in which there are theoretically optimal solutions. Entering the secret garden of good teaching through this well-marked door leads to seeing problems and possibilities in cognitivist terms: as problems of instructional efficiency and representation of subject matter knowledge.

Research and writings about the moral consciousness of teachers, in contrast, are more congruent with the ways teachers themselves see, feel, think, and worry about their relationships with other people's children. This branch of scholarship has great potential, for good and for ill, as it comes to influence teaching, supervision, teacher education, and professional development.

THINKING ABOUT CHILDREN

Usually, educational researchers who wish to influence the shape of teacher education begin by describing, analysing, or experimenting with the work of teachers. But here I wish to start with consideration of children rather than of teachers. Especially with regard to the moral domain, I want to begin with the qualities of children, their needs and vulnerabilities. For, if we know anything at all about the nature of schooling, we know that it is interactive – that each day or week, each moment or year in a classroom is shaped and jointly constructed by teachers and children. Students' personalities, stages of development, language and culture, needs and dreams all pull and guide, shape and limit life in classrooms. It is for this unpredictable drama that we hope to prepare beginners through teacher education and to foster their learning and development through a full and rewarding lifetime.

The first part of our search for good teaching, in Chapter 2, ended in the hands of children, of students; those wise but vulnerable subjects of teachers good and bad, the world over. In the lives of children, teachers are among the most powerful adults on earth. Presidents and prime ministers are distant and mythical characters to children. But, after their parents, teachers hold the greatest real, daily, local power over the quality of life of children in their charge. Parents know this from their own school memories. And in the first minutes of the school year even the youngest children can sense whether the next nine months will be spent closer to heaven or to hell.

When we look at teaching from a child's point of view the buzzing confusion of researchers' claims and counterclaims falls silent. Looking at the faces of particular flesh and blood children, in their need and vulnerability, in their optimism and eagerness, we begin to become humble. For these children, all children, are subjects, not objects. They are not empty vessels to be filled, not animals to be trained, not computers to be programmed, not barbarians to be subdued, disciplined and civilized. All of these metaphors and more have been acted out, with gravely demoralizing effects, on many generations of school-children.

But, for the moment, let us set aside all metaphors and models, theories and habits of mind, that stand between us and the children we are called to serve. What do schoolchildren need? How can teachers begin and continue to meet those needs? And what happens when children's needs are ignored, denied, and discounted by school and society? How might teaching look when seen with sympathy through the eyes of children? Consider these words written in 1992 by a class of adolescents from a Chicago city school as but one desperately honest example of children's eloquence about their needs:

To the Presidential Candidates:

We are students from an inner city high school with 100% African-American enrollment. We represent the part of the US population that feels that some major issues are being overlooked by the candidates. We are the youth of this nation, and we are afraid. You candidates talk about the economy, but that means virtually nothing to us. It is drug sales that regulate the economy in our neighbourhoods, and the political forces we bow to are gangs.

Your proposals on the economy, healthcare and taxes mean little or nothing to people like us, who are hoping merely to stay alive. We hear you talk about straightening out foreign affairs, but we ask you, Which one of you is ready to focus on this country? If you are not going to legalize drugs, then how will you get things under control in our cities? You talk of increasing the number of police, but we know firsthand that that will only waste lives and the taxpayers' money in an endless war. You are asking the impossible in trying to stop the drug trade here; there is simply too much money involved. Besides, what alternative sources of income are being offered to drug dealers if they stop dealing? Which of you candidates will have the government, law enforcement, Big Business, the military and street gangs join together in rebuilding our cities and employing those who have no income other than drug sales? Believe us, gang members and drug dealers are employable: these individuals are already running million-dollar businesses. A joint effort is the only way to save the cities and the US from the drug plague that is destroying minorities today and the rest of the US in the not-so-distant future.

10th Grade Contemporary
American History Class
Lucy Flower High School, Chicago

This letter and these tenth-graders (15-year-olds) are exceptionally eloquent and touching in stating their needs. But their plight is not exceptional. It is sadly typical of the mess enmeshing youth from London to Toronto, New York to Los Angeles, Oslo to Tel Aviv, and many, many more cities, suburbs, and villages in our sophisticated western world. The problems, the needs, failures and partial solutions are moral, not technical or academic. Our children are asking for bread, and we have given them, too often, a stone.

THEORETICAL FRAMEWORK

There are two parts to the theoretical framework within which I think about the moral and ethical dynamics of children in relation to teachers. The first comes from literature, and is beautifully summarized in one page from the Czech writer Milan Kundera's novel *The Joke*. This passage appears late in the story when Ludvik, the main character, realizes that Zemanek, his life-long nemesis, has changed over the last 25 years, to become much more of an ally than an enemy, with political and social views like his own. Here in Kundera's words is the section that tells us something of the kind of problems we face when we begin to deal with changing action in the moral domain:

> There are people who claim to love humanity, while others object that we can love only in the singular, that is, one or another individual. I agree with the latter view and would add that what goes for love goes for hate as well. Man is a being that aspires to equilibrium; he balances the weight of the evil piled on his back with the weight of his hatred. But try concentrating your hatred on mere abstractions – injustice, fanaticism, cruelty – or, if you've gone so far as to find the human principle itself worthy of your hatred, try hating humanity! Hatred on that scale is beyond human capacity, and consequently the only way man can ease his anger (conscious as he is of his limited power) is to concentrate it on an individual.
>
> This is what sent the chill up my spine. Suddenly it occurred to me that from one minute to the next he could point to his metamorphosis (which, it seemed to me, he was suspiciously eager to flaunt) and ask my forgiveness in its name. That was what struck me as so horrible. What would I tell him? How would I respond? How would I explain I couldn't make peace with him? How would I explain it would mean the end of my precarious inner balance? How would I explain it would send one side of my inner scales flying into the air? How would I explain I used my hatred to balance out the weight of the evil I bore as a youth? How would I explain I considered him the embodiment of all the evil I had known? How would I explain I needed to hate him? (p. 229).

So we see that from Kundera's point of view love and hate are individual, specific personal matters, with long and obscure histories in the lives of teachers, parents and children. And that these trajectories are difficult to change, even when we have become aware of their dynamics. Kundera might say 'To know is not enough.'

For the second part of a theoretical framework within which to think about the lives of children, I turn to the work of Alice Miller. She is a former psycho-analyst living and writing in Switzerland. In a series of six books published since

23

1981, Miller makes the argument that children in Western society, your children, my children, are very, very often the victims of child abuse. Yet the victimization of children is denied by society or rationalized as necessary disciplining. Our culture of parenting and pedagogy invariably takes the side of the adult and blames the child for what has been done to him or her; for what was done to you and to me, when we were helpless children. Faced with the power of adults and the social conspiracy of denial, we and our children repress our feelings, idealize or excuse those parents and teachers who abused us, and, tragically, perpetuate the victimization of the next generation. In her six powerful books, ranging from *The Drama of the Gifted Child* (1982) to *Banished Knowledge*(1990), Alice Miller develops, tests, and refines her theory. It is not a happy story. It is not a neutral, cognitivist, abstract picture of human development that she paints. Miller urgently calls for all of us to wake up to the pain that we carry and to the pain that we thoughtlessly but not innocently inflict on children 'for their own good'.

But Alice Miller is not without hope. Her recent work is concerned with how we might break the cycle that she has so poignantly described. And here lies the potential link with our work as teachers. Miller says:

> If mistreated children are not to become criminally oriented or
> mentally ill, it is essential that at least once in their lifetime they
> come into contact with a person who knows without any doubt
> that the environment, not the helpless, battered child, is at fault.
> In this regard, knowledge or ignorance on the part of society can
> be instrumental in either saving or destroying a life. Here lies the
> great opportunity for relatives, social workers, therapists,
> teachers, doctors, psychiatrists, officials, and nurses to support the
> child and to believe her or him (Miller, 1984).

In short, Miller sees the hope of the future in multiplication of those rare and healing moments when a compassionate adult takes a child's pain and dignity seriously, hears the truth, and lets it stand. The most extreme cases of child abuse and its effects that Miller describes are not unknown in ordinary schools. And Miller also argues that normal, sensitive and gifted children are very vulnerable to the kinds of disciplining that is common in British, American and European homes and schools.

I am sorry to report, however, that the programmes of teacher education in which I have taught, and others of which I am aware, do little to prepare tomorrow's teachers for this delicate and compassionate encounter. Instead, the emphasis of teacher training virtually everywhere is typically on behavioural and technical skills and strategies of instruction, cognitive processes like planning and decision-making, and on accumulating knowledge of academic subjects and curriculum materials. Teaching of academic content as rapidly and efficiently as possible is held up as the most important and sometimes the only worthwhile business of schooling. Again and again, national critiques of schooling link the work of teachers to the health of the economy. We are told that we are preparing the next generation of factory workers, scientists and managers, to compete in an unforgiving economic Olympics. Only the brightest, most ruthlessly driven will survive, thrive and taste sweet victory, we are told. Yet, paradoxically, the harder we drive for these laurels, the more elusive individual happiness, cultural stability, and social, moral and mental health become.

I believe that it is time to rethink the ways in which we prepare and educate teachers; to focus more on the moral and ethical dimensions of our vocation. We know from experience and from theorists like Alice Miller that working closely with children is shot through and through with moral implications, each hour and each day. Yet rarely do teacher-educators reveal this, let alone offer useful help in preparing young people for the moral pitfalls and challenges that await them. And rarely are veteran teachers given the support and encouragement we all need to survive our remarkably important vocation.

FUNDAMENTAL NEEDS OF CHILDREN

I do not claim to have all of the answers. I do not have a morally grounded school curriculum or teacher-education programme that I wish to persuade you to adopt. Rather, I want to urge all of us to begin local re-examinations of how we now prepare new teachers and support veterans, how we might in the future, and how we can make better connections between our work and the life needs of the children we are called to serve. One way to begin this process is to consider the fundamental needs of children, and to think about how we might prepare first ourselves, then our replacements, to respond to these fundamental needs.

When I think about the fundamental needs of children, I think first of one special child, my son, Martin Clark. Martin was born in January 1970 and in the spring of that year he began to have epileptic seizures. These seizures of unknown origin were dramatic, uncontrollable and life-threatening. Over time, the effects of several prolonged seizures, together with side effects of powerful but ineffective medications, damaged Martin's brain. At best, he could learn like a 2-year-old. He had very little language, most of which consisted of repetitive words or short phrases. He was energetic and affectionate and completely unafraid of people and the world. Martin became a beautiful boy. At the age of nine-and-a-half, in the month of May, Martin died of heart failure during a seizure.

I think of Martin as my greatest teacher. His patience was legendary, his love unconditional, and he lived in the present moment more intensely than anyone I have ever known. His facial expression concealed nothing – you could always see what he was feeling in his brilliant blue eyes. Through the circumstances of his disease Martin taught me and his mother and his brothers and sisters how to pay deep attention to another human being. I think that we naturally pay this kind of awed attention to newborn infants, so beautiful and innocent and helpless. But with Martin, this continual attending persisted for many years. During that time, he taught me to broaden my sense of what counts as intelligent behaviour – to place less emphasis on language and abstract scientific thought. Martin showed me another way of being with people. As you might guess, he taught me a great deal about myself: what I love and what I fear, what I enjoy and what I resent; about capacities I never imagined I had within me, about my physical and emotional limits; about hope and despair. Martin was a great teacher of children and adults, although he never tried to be.

But there is still another side to my memories of Martin: it seems to me that he had all of the needs that you and I have, and that all children have, in a more visible, available form. His fundamental needs were never masked by self-consciousness or by repression or by training in the adult rituals of politeness. He bore no grudges, he schemed no schemes. His transparent openness made him completely vulnerable. Thinking about Martin led me to compose a short list of fundamental needs of children. I offer this as a place to start in your thinking about how to place our humanness in the foreground as we take better account of the educational opportunities and pitfalls in the moral domain. The basic needs of children are: to be loved, to be led, to be vulnerable, to make sense, to please adults, to have hope, to know truth, to be known, and to be safe. I was urged by my colleague Joseph Featherstone to add a 10th need: to create, to construct, to make one's mark in the local world, to make a difference.

Some day, I suppose, it will be useful to define and illustrate and justify and explain this list of fundamental needs. But I do not propose to do so here and now. For my purpose is to move from considering children and their needs to portraying the moral work faced by teachers, and finally to considering what we may do to help. And before this call is taken to heart, before we even begin to give serious attention to teaching, supervision, and teacher education in the moral domain, we need to show and tell ourselves and those who would teach what to expect, what can go right and go wrong, morally speaking, in classrooms. To that end, I have prepared a table that lists the needs of children and the virtuous responses to each of those needs that every child deserves (see Table 3.1). Along with these, I have also listed the dark side of life in classrooms: the temptations that the relative powerlessness and vulnerability of children present to all teachers at different times, and a partial list of commonplace ways that I have seen and experienced abuse in school, at the hands of well-meaning teachers. Read these lists. See if you can remember examples of virtuous responses to your needs as a child. And also try to remember a time when you were hit with exactly the negative opposite of what you needed. Speaking for myself, these were the educational events that changed and shaped my life. These are the facts and cases and feelings that I shall remember long after the algebra and the chemistry are forgotten. These are the little moments when mental health hangs in the balance. Yet the teacher-educators whom I know rarely, if ever, speak of these matters; rarely even tell their students that their thoughts, feelings and actions

Table 3.1. Needs of children, virtuous and negative responses

Needs of children	*Virtuous response*	*Temptations*	*Common manifestation*
To be loved	Unconditional love	Condition love; Emotional and sexual exploitation	Favoritism; seduction; physical and sexual abuse
To be led	Empowerment	Enslavement	Total and punitive control
To be vulnerable	Kindness	Cruelty	Humiliation
To make sense	Justice; fairness	Arbitrariness	Authoritarianism
To please others	Humility; patience	Anger; pride	Outbursts of temper
To have hope	Hope	Despair	Cynicism
To know truth	Honesty	Dishonesty	Lying; denial
To be known	Respect	Contempt	Disrespect; sarcasm
To be safe	Responsibility	Indifference; dereliction	Irresponsibility; blaming the victim
To make one's mark	Authentic work; autonomy	Narcissism; egocentrism	Inauthentic work; hypercriticality; taking credit for children's work

in the moral domain will be the most problematic, the most rewarding and among the most consequential of their lives.

IMPLICATIONS FOR TEACHER EDUCATION

Now we have a delicate problem before us. We know something about the moral possibilities and pitfalls of teaching children that the teachers of tomorrow do not yet know. But it is one thing to point out a danger or an opportunity, and quite another to do something about it. For a while, at least, it seems that ignorance is bliss. But I, for one, cannot go back, cannot forget the lessons that Alice Miller and Martin Clark have taught me. My urgent question is 'What can we do'?

For an answer, I look to two sources. First, I turn to history, to remember and reflect on the means that human civilizations and societies have invented and refined, over thousands of years, to protect themselves from moral harm. My search yielded a list of seven time-honoured ways of dealing with temptations: 1) naming the pitfalls; 2) self-examination; 3) study of moral literatures; 4) practice of moral disciplines; 5) doing good; 6) confession with forgiveness; and 7) membership in a caring community. As you may infer, these means have developed in connection with organized religion, which is sometimes subject to problems of dogmatic control and 'moralizing' rather than the forms of moral thought and action that we hope to encourage in teachers. Yet, I think that we can learn from those who have gone before and shape some of their inventions to our educational purposes.

The second source to which I turn for part of an answer is our current literature about and knowledge of the best practices of teacher education. My guess and my hope are that, in small ways, for reasons only partly understood, the seeds of solution to the challenge of preparing morally thoughtful teachers already have begun to germinate in particular teachers colleges, induction programmes, and in special relationships between universities and schools. Good teachers are being educated, here and there. It is up to us to learn how to see and do likewise by framing our educational problem in terms of cultivating moral development, nurturing a caring spirit, and practising active compassion for children.

NAMING THE PITFALLS

For example, let's look at several of the seven historical ways of dealing with temptations, and see how current or possible directions in teacher education match up (see Table 3.2). First, consider the principle of 'naming the pitfalls'. In classical moral literature and tradition, and in contemporary law, it is essential to name and describe what constitutes error, what counts as a moral transgression, what we should beware of. Without a name, without an explicit warning, there can be no fair expectation of moral responsibility. But even beyond responsibility, we cannot expect to see, hear, or feel moral issues or opportunities if we have no word, no language, no medium that puts boundaries around the event. This is particularly true for those of us who would teach, warn, or prepare the young for moral territory unknown to them. In contemporary writings about teaching and teacher education I see some promising starts to Eve's and Adam's task of naming all things. My friend Robert Yinger has written persuasively about the need to develop a 'language of practice' with which teachers can see, think, feel, and deliberate more richly and profitably (Yinger, 1987). A book edited by Goodlad, Soder, and Sirotnik, *The Moral Dimensions of Teaching* (1990), provides the germ of a philosophical and empirical vocabulary for educators who wish to see what we've so long ignored. This chapter, together with the

Table 3.2. Time-honoured ways for dealing with temptation

1. Naming the pitfalls	Language of practice
2. Self-examination	Reflection
3. Study of moral literatures	Moral cases
4. Practice moral disciplines	Retreat; rituals
5. Doing good	Community service
6. Confession with forgiveness	Support groups
7. Membership in a caring community	Cohort

work of Alice Miller, will, I hope, contribute to the beginnings of naming the evils, and to discussing them openly. The first step to educating the good teacher requires better moral charts for the teacher, naming and locating the hazards to navigation.

CONFESSION WITH FORGIVENESS

Next, consider the principle of 'confession with forgiveness' or, in more secular terms, acceptance in spite of our failings. By this I mean the social mechanism for hope in a fallible existence. Some of us have lived in or come to know about a family or a village, or a school or a society in which to confess a mistake, a weakness, a failure brings punishment and rejection. 'One mistake and you're dead' is the way my wife describes such situations. In such circumstances, people become fearful, controlling, dishonest and secretive. This is even more the case when punishment comes for errors of belief, thought, or ideology. But when an ethos of acceptance has been cultivated, you and I are free to admit our mistakes, to substitute learning from experience for the fear of retribution, and to receive moral support for avoiding such mistakes in future. In teacher education and teacher development projects with veteran teachers I and others (e.g. Cavazos, 1994; McConaghy, 1991; Featherstone *et al.*, 1993) have been developing a forum called 'professional development support groups'. The purpose of these informal meetings is for teachers to have a safe and supportive audience for their stories, cautionary tales, questions, and personal dilemmas. The ground rules for participation include no interruptions, no advice giving, and no telling of these stories outside the group. Within these groups, we learn to listen, to tell stories with a point, to see our dilemmas in a wider perspective. While not intended as therapy or to focus only on difficulties, I've found that teachers take great comfort from being able to articulate their worries and concerns to a group of fellow professionals who understand and sympathize, and do not judge or punish. Often, teachers discover that an embarrassing secret they have carried heavily on their conscience is common, ordinary, and quickly let go. I think that we ought to experiment with beginning such educative conversations early in the process of becoming a teacher and with building them into the weekly pattern of life at school.

STUDY MORAL LITERATURE

A third defence against temptation is 'study of moral literature'. By this I mean the stories, parables, poems, biographies, myths and proverbs that use narrative to make the abstract vivid and memorable. As Joseph Campbell said: 'A myth is something that never happened, yet occurs daily' (Campbell with Moyers, 1988). The uses of story, song, and verse are more than efficient memory aids for the illiterate. From literature, good literature, we partake of the experience of another. In our imaginations we merge with a character in a drama, feel his pain, her joy; see through their eyes and, for a time, breathe to their rhythm. Good literature draws us beyond the compass of our everyday horizons, to places near to heart and far from home. It makes us think and feel and be someone else for a while. Powerful literature exercises our capacity to take the perspective of another human being. Perspective taking is essential to moral thought and behaviour.

Teaching and teacher education cry out for good literature. Some teacher-educators use films like *Dead Poets' Society* or *Educating Rita* to make the moral risks and promises of teaching more palpable. Autobiographies of teachers and novels about schooling, from *Goodbye, Mr. Chips* to *Anne of Green Gables*, can also serve these ends, as can the telling of our own autobiographical tales to those who would follow us. And case studies of moral issues in education have begun to appear, some of which are retold in Part III of this book.

SELF-EXAMINATION

Advocating the discipline of self-examination in teaching and teacher education is quite popular today, with terms like 'reflection' and 'contemplation' conspicuous in the titles of numerous books and articles. In the case before us, the issue is not whether teachers should be encouraged to be reflective, but rather what we should encourage them to be reflective about. Self-examination in the moral domain requires that we step outside ourselves and honestly compare our actions with some standard or communally sanctioned expectations for moral behaviour. This takes courage, community support and practice. Self-examination is easy to postpone, especially when our intuition tells us that the task and its consequences will be uncomfortable. And, ironically, the typical organization of testing and evaluation in schooling perpetuates this reluctance to practice self-examination. Valid and reliable examinations, we are told by the psychometricians, must be objective and done by an unbiased other; by an authority figure with mysterious expertise. But are we not trying to influence teachers and children to be independent of our supervision, confident, capable of good judgement and self-control, eager for responsibility, and willing to learn and improve with experience? If so, we should introduce self-examination early and practise often in teacher education curriculum and in the staff room of every school.

CARING COMMUNITY

Finally, consider the role of membership in a caring community as a means to educate and sustain the thoughtful teacher. Teaching is typically a solitary, even lonely profession. One teacher is, more often than not, alone and in charge of 20 to 30 children. Differences in age, status, knowledge, and responsibility separate the teacher from the society of the taught, even in the most egalitarian schools. The very privacy and independence that come with the closing of the classroom door can also have a high cost in terms of energy, perspective, and alienation. Physical and moral burnout can come from such isolation. One antidote to these problems is active membership in a caring community of fellow professionals. Communities develop, change and enforce norms and traditions, provide a place for each member and a support system. In the best of circumstances, caring communities perform the rituals of induction, initiation, celebration and grieving that honour the identity and worth of each and all.

In large colleges of education in America, almost by accident, communities of the kind described here have been formed within each class of prospective teachers. Future teachers are grouped into 'cohorts' of from 25 to 65 students. They take courses together, participate in common field experiences, student teaching and social events for two years. The cohort effects can include forming close bonds with fellow teachers, practice at professional discourse, and learning how the minds and emotions of others work over long periods of time. I believe that to give proper attention to the moral issues raised here will require a cohort approach both for the short run of a two-year teacher education programme, and also as a model for how veteran teachers might organize themselves – for mutual moral support, as a context for learning how to listen, for questioning one's own situation, and for digging deeper than the surface appearances to the level of moral deliberation and action.

A MODEL OF MORAL EXPERTISE

It is our challenge and our duty to experiment with these and other proposed means to the end of enhanced ethical sensitivity by teachers. At the same time, I believe we require a new definition or model of ethical expertise to guide our designs. Perhaps we should consider the developmental model proposed by Dreyfus and Dreyfus (1990). They describe a five-stage process of movement towards moral maturity, ranging from novice, through advanced beginner, competence, proficiency, to expertise. A distinctive feature of their theory is that the highest two stages do not depend on intellectual judgement and deliberate decision-making for ethical coping (in contrast to the more intellectualized theories of Piaget and Kohlberg). The morally proficient person doesn't decide what is right, she sees what is right. The moral expert does the right thing intuitively and immediately, without deliberation or analysis. To reach these highest states of moral action (not just clever judgement) requires experience, practice, and attention to feelings of satisfaction or regret. All of these, in turn, require a moral vocabulary and a community of care beginning, perhaps, at our teachers' colleges.

CONCLUSION

I hope that I have heightened your concern about the moral dimension of education by highlighting the perspective of the child. Good things can happen between students and teachers, and bad things can happen. In a sense, the most insidious bad things that can happen are the most common and ordinary – the taken for granted classroom events that break the spirit, blame the victim, and make cruelty seem reasonable. Our own survival of such experiences does not excuse them, let alone recommend them to the next generation. Our mere humanity entitles us to better treatment than we received, and this is so for our children and our teacher education students as well.

We cannot solve all of the problems of educating good teachers in a few easy steps. But we ought to make a beginning, by showing ourselves and our students the moral pitfalls and the moral opportunities that everywhere surround us. In our teacher education programmes and in our work with veteran teachers, in our reading, teaching, and research, we can ask what it would take to form cohorts, to develop an ethos of acceptance and care, to practise constructive self-examination, and to read and help create a literature of moral cases.

Preparation for coping with the moral dilemmas of teaching is possible and necessary. Ignoring these challenges has not made them go away. If the cycle of morally insensitive pedagogy does not begin to end with our generation, where will it end? And if we, who now know something of the moral dimension of teaching, return to business as usual, a golden opportunity will slip away.

PART TWO

RESEARCH AND THOUGHTFUL TEACHING

Section Two is a three-part apologia for my stance towards research as a teacher and towards teaching as a researcher. I call this section 'Research *and* Thoughtful Teaching' to emphasize that I am exploring a two-sided, two-way relationship between people, ideas and ways of understanding. The first chapter, 'Connecting Teachers and Research', is in the somewhat unconventional form of an interview transcript. John Zeuli, a friend and colleague of mine, interviewed me as part of his research project on teachers' conceptions of research. During our conversation I spelled out some pretty strong beliefs about how I try to help make constructive connections between teachers and that mixed literature called 'educational research'.

'Research in the Service of Teaching' is a revision of a speech that I gave to a conference of teachers in 1984. I've updated some of the examples, but the basic argument is as true now as it was ten years ago: both teachers and researchers will find additional benefits in educational research when we stop thinking of research as an impersonal compendium of 'right answers'. Instead, the thoughtful teacher selectively draws from research and researchers all manner of information, inspiration, vision and support, in doing the ultimately local work of good teaching.

Finally, 'Real Lessons from Imaginary Teachers' is a set of reflections on the unusual, perhaps unique, case of Susan Hall, a thoughtful teacher who became a research collaborator with not one but two qualitative researchers, during two different school years. What can we learn from the story of the twice-studied teacher, about research, about representing the lives of others, and about the inevitable changes resulting from teachers saying 'yes' to researchers?

Chapter 4

Connecting Teachers and Research[1]

John: There are two topics concerning teachers and research that I'd like you to address: teachers' dispositions towards research, and teachers' conceptual understandings of research.

Chris: For me John, the most helpful distinction is between what teachers think about and feel about *research as a process* on the one hand, and their understanding, appreciation of, and use of particular research studies on the other hand. Teachers hold preconceptions about a distant activity and community called 'research' that they've had some exposure to; often an exposure that makes them feel inadequate. These notions about what research is and is not, and teachers' feelings when they are thrown into direct contact with research or researchers can undermine the second part of what I'm interested in, which is teachers coming to a place where they can make use of some of the fruits of research on the ways teaching and learning work.

     Until teachers' preconceptions about research are taken seriously I don't have much hope that they will become disposed to be thoughtful about making connections between what researchers know and what teachers might do about their own understanding and action. When I teach a workshop or course with teachers I introduce myself as a researcher. I publish and I do research, and I speak that language. But I also violate every part of the stereotype of the researcher who is insensitive to practice, who uses technical language in a way that confuses or excludes people who aren't insiders. I present myself as a counterexample to the stereotype of the researcher who treats or thinks of teachers as the inferior partner in the relationship.

John: I think about my interview data with teachers, in which they would say all types of negative things about researchers.

'They live in an ivory tower. They are not concerned about what we do. We can't understand what the articles mean, and no one helps us understand them.' You present yourself as someone who is in that ivory tower, but does not support the stereotype of the ivory tower researcher.

Chris: That's right, I try. At least, I am an existence proof that *one* researcher doesn't fit this stereotype, and that this one researcher spends unstructured time in public school classrooms, gets down and dirty in the apple sauce when the kids are making apple sauce, is a parent of school-age kids, a booster of the band and orchestra, a person who knows from direct experience and values what teachers are doing day in and day out, and celebrates the wisdom of practice. There's a second part to this besides violating the stereotype of the researcher. I also violate the stereotype of the teacher! That is, I challenge the image of teachers being practical and hard-working, tired but not wise, and lacking valid and valuable experiences worthy of being called 'wisdom'.

John: Do you mean that as you take the role of a teacher, you're someone who sees the value of that role, whereas some teachers might not see the value in what they're doing or of what they know?

Chris: That's right. I both exemplify it, and show and tell them that *they* exemplify it. It's not only a matter of identification, of me joining them. The second part is just as important and a little more subtle: the invitation for them to join me as equal partners with complementary, different, but equally valuable knowledge, skills, dispositions, perspectives, even theories. The character of teachers' theories is different from the character of theory in social science, but much of what teachers do and believe is theoretically guided. It's the difference between a formal theory and an implicit theory, a kind of personal, practical knowledge as Jean Clandinin[2] would say.

That teachers are theoreticians, however defined, is a quite powerful claim. Their theories can be articulated, and made even sharper for thinking deeply about what they're doing and seeing. Teachers' theories have the same uses as theory does in science: understanding, predicting, and controlling. So, at the end of this conversation, whether it takes an hour or two weeks, we (teachers and researchers) are in the same boat. We teachers and we researchers are, for the sake of schoolchildren, engaged in thought and action, aimed at understanding, predicting and influencing what kids know, remember, and can do.

John: It sounds like you're saying, on the one hand, these are some of the problems teachers have in thinking about research in general, and that you want to break down their fears. You want to reassure teachers that we can be one of you, and you can be one of us.

Chris: And to support that by saying that their experience to date is valid. I am not saying to a teacher, 'You got it wrong, research has always been an enterprise that has your interests at heart.' I'm saying, you're right, you probably had a terrible humiliating experience if you took a course in educational statistics in a Master's program, or if you were forced to read reports of research in an undergraduate educational psychology course that you didn't understand, and it seemed in the final analysis to be complicating common sense, instead of giving you helpful insight. You're right about that. But it doesn't have to be that way. You don't need to write off the entire enterprise of research as a window for understanding and guiding your action on the basis of those unhappy experiences that you might have had.

John: In other words, why they feel sceptical and wary is understandable and reasonable. But, might some teachers also feel negative toward research because they fundamentally misunderstand what research can and cannot do?

Chris: Sure. I think they're connected as well. We now get to the distinction between research as an enterprise, as a way of apprehending the world through an inquiry-oriented attitude and technology. And of a pragmatic view of the function of research, not the process, but what it is a conception about. Ideas about what research is for. And what I've been talking about so far is the process orientation, the inquiry disposition, and also some of the language problems and impediments to teachers joining that conversation.

I think that teachers, whether they've had good experiences or bad with research, can still hold beliefs about what research is for that are wrong or unhelpful. The beliefs that I find very common and very unhelpful are that research is for finding answers or research is for solving problems; or that research is for discovering and proving what the guaranteed, effective ways are of doing things.

Research shows, research proves, research solves my problems. Just tell me what you spent a million dollars finding out so I can take this pill and never make a mistake again, because you researchers have done the hard work of finding the best way to teach reading or science. And I trust you. I'm not smart enough to question you.

That complex of beliefs about what research is for is a big impediment to entering into reflective inquiry oneself, examining one's own practice and one's own local world in a systematic way. And it's also a set-up for making negative judgments about the research you come into contact with. Because research never does come up with the kind of categorical final answers human nature wishes for. Research, when it's done well, doesn't make your life easier. It makes it more complex as a teacher. It gives you even more to think about.

John: So that attitude would subvert any positive relationship with research.

Chris: Exactly. It creates a parent-child relationship between researchers and teachers. 'It's true because the data and I said so, that's why. We researchers said so, and we have the authority to prove it, but you don't understand data anyway, so just take our word for it.'

John: And often is seems like it is in the researchers' interest to present what they're doing in that light. They want to be seen as wise experts making important discoveries. These are cultural norms about what people who are getting money and doing science should be providing. It's hard to resist that, and to criticize it.

Chris: That's right, and it's very seductive from both sides: from the side of the researcher who wants to win the Nobel Prize, and from the side of the teacher who says, 'Well at least somebody is taking care of the complexity. One of these days they are going to solve all my problems and life will be easy.' And we use unhelpful analogies to medical researchers finding the vaccine that prevents polio as a partially understood model for what educational research could or should be. Culturally there is what I would call an inappropriate generalization from physical and medical science to research in education that leads people to promise and hope for cures and breakthroughs that will make life easier and more efficient and filled with leisure and joy.

John: Okay. That's helpful to me because I wanted to have you discuss something I've been thinking about. Teachers' disposition to see research as proving things or solving classroom problems seems to be a major impasse. But, what you've talked about in terms of how teachers should be helped to see research doesn't meet this problem head on. Your approach might help, but it seems like this problem has to be met head on. Have you given some thought about that?

Chris: Yes. What I'm talking about is a three-stage process. We've been talking about the first stage, which is coming to some common ground, opening minds and eyes and conversations that permit the possibility that research has *something* to offer to teachers that isn't recipes and solutions. Without that common ground, and without some challenge of unhelpful stereotypes in both directions, you can't get to stage two or three.

   Stage two involves me and a few teachers, working together on a specific case or example of research, and taking it apart and putting it back together again. It doesn't have to be a good example. It can be an example that lives up to all the stereotypes of unhelpful language, strangely construed questions and hypotheses, and mysterious statistical analysis. That can work just as well as something clear and beautiful, maybe even better. Because what we do is read this and ask a different set of questions about it than you would typically be asked if you were reading it for a college course. Instead we ask, 'What experiences as teachers have you had that are instances of, or confirmed by, or challenged by what we've read here?' So, at the very outset we're saying *you* have something to bring: an interpretive framework of your experience as a teacher that you can connect to what these researchers tell us they did and learned. Let's get your experience on the table as a powerful, valid, incomplete, rich ground from which to interpret this text. And interpret this text as the story told in a telegraphic fashion about experiences some researchers had in some classrooms.

   Another line of questions might be, 'What food for thought, what questions worth asking about your own school, your own self, your own students, your own way of doing things are evoked by reading this instance of research and discussing it with other teachers and with me? What conceptual categories, ideas, ways of putting boundaries around things that happen at school are you reminded of or put into contact with for the first time by the reading and in the conversation that we've had, and how might those be usable as lenses for you to describe your past experience as a teacher and observer of children, or for the future as something to look through, a new or dusted off way of describing and seeing practice?'

You do that a few times, and we don't even worry about the formally stated results, the findings, the prescriptions for how to behave that typically wind up an article. What we're doing is a form of close reading of the text in the context of the collective and individual experiences of the teachers. We are acting on some of the abstract principles that I talked about in phase one: That your experience is valuable, that the language of research and its methods of inquiry are also valuable and different. That there are multiple ways to make the link between research and practice other than simply accepting on blind faith the prescriptions that might typically be claimed as 'findings and implications'.

John: But I could imagine a teacher doing all that and saying, 'Well, I understand what this person is saying about reading comprehension. I understand the basic concept, though I don't understand all the fancy terms he is using. I understand that they want me to ask more thought provoking questions of my students. But my experience is that when you ask all these questions, problems emerge. And I feel from my experience that I handle reading very well, and I don't really understand how this can be valuable to me. What process are you trying to get me to do? How can I read this? Do you want to look beyond this one article? Is there a set of questions you want me to ask of *every* article that will enhance what I do? I don't buy that because I feel very comfortable about what I do, and I feel quite distant from this.'

Chris: I hear you saying two or three things. One is, Are you trying to get me (the teacher) to agree that I have a new responsibility to keep up with the literature? That I have a responsibility that I haven't been discharging, which is to read a lot more research and to go through this kind of process that we've just played with, of finding questions and conceptual categories, and complicating my life by reading the latest on reciprocal teaching of reading? Or maybe even turning things upside down in my classroom by trying to institute a new system of instruction in the middle of the year?

No, John, I am not saying that. I'm saying, learning to interpret research can be like taking painting lessons. You don't have to become a painter for the rest of your life or work that into your daily routine in order to get your money's worth from adult education. But once you've been through the demystification of the process of painting or interpreting research, you are *capable* of doing something you weren't capable of before. It's still your decision about how you act on this new knowledge you have of yourself and a body of literature.

I do believe that thoughtful reflection on one's own practice is an excellent path to teaching in a personally satisfying way. I won't go so far as to say it's the only responsible way, but I'll come close to that. Here is a tool, a set of ways of seeing, thinking, reading and discourse that supports and stands for what I mean by thoughtful and responsible teaching. Now you are beginning to know what I mean, know some of the costs as well as the benefits. I and others can testify to the benefits of having a richer, more funny, engaging way to see your own life, to see the amazing in what yesterday was ordinary.

I respect teachers enough to say, 'It's your life to decide how to live. If you choose to continue teaching in the ways that you have always taught, then you've chosen that.' That's the mark of a professional: the freedom to make choices of that kind. That freedom is in tension with professional responsibilities that teachers take on, and which pull you more toward complexity and reflection and analysis, and creatively responsible change on your part, as well as on the part of your students. What we're doing here is tasting the water of sensemaking in a genre of text that represents what researchers typically have to offer, with a new set of spices, a new set of techniques and attitudes about what's in this for me, what I can use this tool for, what other things I can use it for than what we typically assume and learn in college, or even in graduate programmes.

In any case, what I mean by phase two is the experience of making unconventional use of conventional research. It works even better when it's the teachers who bring in the examples, the kinds of research, the kinds of journals and magazines that they find in their school libraries or whatever other sources they might have. That way there's

41

often a topical interest. It's about reading or maths, or middle schools that they've got some interest in or ownership of. And then we say, 'Let's see what we can do with this.'

John: What you've said makes me think that you're trying to change the content of the faith they should have in researchers. They should no longer believe that research can provide them with direct techniques.

Chris: Or answers: the one right way to do things.

John: What they should believe is that research can help them become more reflective about what they do.

Chris: And to find local answers to locally defined puzzles, problems, and dilemmas. What I'm advocating is a local, situational, practitioner-driven, problem solving, problem finding, dilemma management strategy that can be helped along by what researchers have discovered in the few cases that they've studied, and with the tools they've selected, and with the techniques they've used, and within the conceptual frames and theories they've invented. But, the buck doesn't stop with the researchers being wise and articulate and prescriptive. The buck stops with the English teacher at a local high school who has a problem, or a challenge, or an opportunity, or a question that might have been raised by or enriched or framed by practical experience, or theory and research. And the problem or challenge must be, I think, pursued by the teacher on the scene, drawing help from me as a consultant, or another teacher as a helper, or maybe from something published in *Reading Research Quarterly*. There are all kinds of potentially helpful ideas and materials, but the teacher still remains the centre stage problem solver, dilemma manager, change agent. The researcher is too removed in space and time from the school, the community, and the high school class of juniors taking English III.

   So, it's not only a fundamental difference in the way in which teachers view research and researchers. It also requires a fundamental change in how they view themselves. And that's why I say that thoughtful teaching promises to complicate their lives if they take it seriously.

John: Because they'll view themselves and what they do in a more complex way.

Chris: Right. And their responsibilities as extending farther afield than before.

John: That's painful, potentially painful for them.

Chris: It is.

John: So you're seducing them in the first phase. The second phase . . .

Chris: The second phase is still seduction, in a way, because there's a thrill associated with understanding something for the first time, and with feeling some power over what was formerly an opportunity to feel embarrassed, and feel inadequate, and apologetic for your own experience. The third phase is the hard one. That's the 'go forth and become a researcher on your own practice' stage.

John: In my own research, I've seen two different kinds of responses of teachers to research. Some teachers believe that research should give answers. Others will say that research provides me with ideas I can think about. But what troubles me about the latter group is that research provides them with all these ideas that they could put into a hat. And they could stick their hand in and pick out any idea and think about it. But the ideas are in isolation, and they have little to do with how the researchers have contextualized the ideas and justified their value or lack of value. In other words, this second group of teachers are unaware of the standards that are part of different types of research. Understandably so, but I think problematically so too. What do you think about that?

Chris: Okay. So, that approach can lead to a kind of a willy-nilly, cut-and-paste, decontextualized, and potentially harmful misuse of what otherwise could be appropriately qualified and contextualized research.

John: 'One idea is as good as another if it's something I'm interested in, seems relevant, and is something I can understand.' That's a key problem.

Chris: The way I answer that John, is with a metaphor. We can think about research as published as we think about a set of encyclopedia. We don't use an encyclopedia by starting on the first page of volume A and reading all the way to Z, nor do we open a volume at any old page and hope to be enlightened. Rather, we use an encyclopedia when we have a need for information about a topic that arises from practice, from life. We go through an indexing system to a place where the information is put in a compact but contextualized form. And we draw from that tiny subpart of the whole encyclopedia selectively, and in a way that we hope gives an appreciation of the larger context within which this information resides.

So, rather than your metaphor of the hat with little slips of paper in it with research findings written on them, what we have in that hat or in that encyclopedia is a condensed, but more comprehensive and contextualized body of work. One particular study or idea maybe be featured, may include a key idea that you or I could make use of today. I'm saying to teachers that we're practicing a fuzzing of the boundaries, a moving away from the 'magic pill' notion that you can find just the right sentence, word or procedure to solve your problem. You may take that away from it, but you also come away with a richer understanding of where it came from, how it fits into a larger framework of inquiry that continues, that's ongoing.

John: So, it is a matter of contextualizing the issue.

Chris: Right, which is also a professional responsibility. You can't just use the tool without reading the directions. And the directions include where it came from, where it's headed, and where it fits in the larger picture.

John: It's also a matter of contrasting your own experience with the standards that are part of the claims of the article. That's a very difficult problem.

Chris: It is. It is. That's a real difficult problem.

John: And it seems to me one of the ways to address it is to help teachers to become willing to ask questions about that. And your responsibility as a researcher is to answer as accurately and understandably as possible.

Chris: That's right. It's a disposition to be self-critical in the best sense of the word 'critical'. To be analytic about your own experience. There's a wonderful book, called *Human inference: Strategies and shortcomings of social judgment*,[3] in which Richard Nisbett and Lee Ross point out how often people give themselves the benefit of the doubt. How, for example, we tend to pay attention to positive instances of things we were expecting to happen, and be insensitive to the absence of things we weren't expecting. And therefore we come up with skewed judgements about how important or frequent x is compared to y. They're talking about fundamental qualities of human thought and behaviour, dispositions and patterns that contrast with the canons of evidence, the standards of justified true belief that scientists make explicit and worry about.

What I am promising to teachers is that if you take the step of moving toward a more examined approach to your own life, and if you agree to borrow from research, in selective and sometimes creative ways, you'll be able to do more good for the students with whom you work. You'll probably be less bored and less subject to burnout. You will feel more powerful and more healthy about your intellectual life and your work as a teacher or a parent, and about the sense you make of your own history as a student and teacher. I'm talking about raising the probability of doing good from what it is today to what it can be tomorrow if you begin this journey. And it is not a one-time conversion. It's the beginning of a process, the beginning of a slow, complicated, and recursive process. It's not a promise to fix anything, or improve everything about your life as a teacher in one stroke. It's the continuation of the preparation of yourself to become a more thoughtful teacher. No matter how many years of experience you have, I'm asking you to return to preparation, to continually prepare yourself as a habit of mind and as a way of becoming.

John: You were going to talk about that third phase.

Chris: In a way we have gotten into it already, John. If you accept my offer to move in the direction of this kind of an examined life and relationship to research as one contribution to that way of seeing, that way of being, then you've moved into phase three. The way I've operationalized that in a two-week course, is to ask teachers to write a proposal for a self-directed professional development project that they have some hope of starting during the next school year. What aspect of my work do I want help with, do I want to understand better, in my own interest and in the interest of my students? I ask them to write this proposal in the form of a letter to some person in their local school authority who could approve it and give them the resources that will help make this come true: time, materials, or consultation with others. So, they are also learning to make their professional

45

development a proactive and collective part of the life of the school for the coming year.

John: So, how does writing that proposal relate specifically to research?

Chris: It *is* a type of research itself, and I also stipulate that they show the audience of that proposal how published research has been and can be helpful in pulling off what they propose. They must cite particular articles and programmes of research that helped frame their problem and define it, that offer tools to experiment with, whether those be methods or approaches to teaching, or that offer methods of inquiry – ways of keeping track of the cause-effect relationships that the teacher/researcher intends to understand more deeply.

John: What if in the proposal a teacher presents research as providing answers for the school district for increasing mathematics achievement? This would be a common sense approach to the task.

Chris: Remember these are people who have had from two to ten weeks experience discussing the nature and limits of research, and they have had an opportunity to present a draft of the proposal and get feedback from me and from others. In the hypothetical example you gave, my feedback would be, 'can I help you reframe this not as answers, but as an experiment worth pursuing where the real challenge is for you in this school or in this district to try out a set of ideas pioneered elsewhere and really see how it suits you?' Not just buy it, guaranteed with the Good Housekeeping Seal of Approval. But, make the case that this looks like it's worth trying on the basis of the experience of others elsewhere.

And, as wise consumers, we need to set up a way of adapting, accommodating it, and locally determining what the costs and benefits are. We can find good solid nominations of things to try and ways to behave in the experience of others, including researchers. But, I would try to bring them back around to the idea that we're not sure they are answers *for us* until we've tried these answers *in context*, and paid attention to the intended effect, and the side effects, and the surprises, the disappointments and the costs. So, a year from now we may be able to say that was a good answer for our situation, but we can't tell that in advance. We can only tell what looks like a good bet.

John: In other words, when you come to that point in the course, you have already tried to dissuade them from that type of simplistic look at the problem.

Chris: Yes. But you're right, you have to be alert to it because all of us will regress to old habits and ways of thinking.

John: All this has been very helpful to me. It helped confirm what I saw as a major problem.

Chris: Which one?

John: Teachers' disposition to look at research for definitive answers. And it also gave me some ideas to think about for changing that.

Chris: I'm glad we got to phase three together.

NOTES

1   This interview was conducted by John Zeuli on 13 March 1990 at East Lansing, MI, as part of his dissertation 'How do teachers understand research when they read it?' (see also Zeuli, 1994).

2   D. Jean Clandinin, a professor of teacher education at the University of Alberta, has done ground breaking work on teachers' personal practical knowledge and on storytelling as a medium for articulating teacher knowledge.

3   Nisbett, R. and Ross, L. (1980) *Human inference: Strategies and shortcomings of social judgment*. Englewood Cliffs, NJ: Prentice-Hall.

Chapter 5

*Research in the Service of Teaching

This chapter is addressed to both teachers and educational researchers. My message is an optimistic one, namely, that research on teaching and school learning can be even more useful to practising teachers than it has been in the past. To realize this, teachers and researchers must begin to think more flexibly and creatively about the nature and roles of educational research, the needs of the practical world of schools and classrooms, and about new ways in which their two communities can communicate in mutually helpful ways. The chapter is divided into four sections, each headed by an exhortation: 'Let's get humble!, Let's demand service!, Let's get creative!, and Let's get communicating! I hope that your responses to these exhortations will move us toward more inspired use of educational research in the service of teaching.

LET'S GET HUMBLE!

Like many virtues, humility is a great deal easier to prescribe than to practise. As John Wesley said, 'It is difficult to be humble. Even if you aim at humility, there is no guarantee that when you have attained the state you will not be proud of the feat.' When I call for humility in connection with research on teaching what I am urging is a more modest sense of proportion about the size and scope of what social science has to offer. In research proposals and in the introductions to textbooks educational researchers often claim that the fundamental bedrock of effective teaching is, or should be, empirical research. 'Research-based' is a much sought-after prefix for texts, curricula, and teacher education programmes. The old saying 'To the carpenter, the world is made of wood' can also be applied to social scientists who tend to value teaching to the extent that it reflects their own discoveries.

But in my view, teaching is not primarily an applied science. Rather, teaching is a complex, social, personal, political and interactive human process. Empirical research on teaching and learning can be one element of what a teacher takes into account in his or her planning and teaching, but only one of many. Research can *inform* practice but research – because of self-imposed constraints – can be much too narrow or too tightly bounded and controlled to literally serve as a *foundation* for practice.

I believe it would help us all to be more appropriately humble about the role of research in informing practice if we were to take some of the mystery out of the research process. People have a tendency to be somewhat awed by very complex research designs, analysis methods and jargon-laden reports of results. Sometimes the complexity is necessary and the special technical terms crucial for precise expression of meaning. But meaning is obscured and potential usefulness to teachers reduced by unnecessarily complex designs and excessive use of technical terminology.

It helps to reduce the mystery surrounding research in education when I remind myself that, when you boil them down, all research reports consist of descriptions of researchers' experiences and ideas. These experiences and ideas may be expressed in numbers or in words, more or less clearly, but there is always a person or group of persons behind the words and numbers. And these persons, the researchers, are not inaccessible beings set apart and somehow quite different from the other members of the community of educators. On the whole, they are quite willing to return telephone calls, respond to letters, and come to conferences to talk, to listen, to learn and to teach. So perhaps one of the most valuable resources we have as a profession is access to dedicated and intelligent people who have spent years thinking about, observing and writing about topics and situations of importance to educators.

At the same time, it is important to remember that the world's foremost expert on a particular classroom or school setting is the teacher in that setting. The experience and expertise of a teacher may sometimes be enhanced or helpfully focused by drawing on the experiences of others outside the classroom. But, in the final analysis, the teacher is the planner, decision-maker, and actor who has the most intimate knowledge of and greatest influence in his or her classroom. Teaching, like research, can be a constructively humbling experience.

LET'S DEMAND SERVICE!

The idea that the main role of research and researchers is to *serve* teachers is new, and has not yet swept through the profession like wildfire. The concept of service is not well developed yet, and traditional ideas about service are at odds with the relatively high status and authority that researchers enjoy. But for teachers to be able to make more appropriate use of research and researchers' experience, we need a richer, more positive conception of service. Part of this new notion of service will have to be worked out between individual researchers and teachers. What I have to offer is a list of four ways in which research on teaching, and the researchers themselves, might serve teachers. The four modes of service are: information, inspiration, vision and support.

Information

The most typical way in which research has served the practice of teaching is by providing information. The journals are full of descriptions of how teaching and learning worked under various conditions and in various settings. Most of this information is presented at a general level, having been derived from the averaging of many observations of many individuals or classes. And most of the information found in the research literature pertains to specific questions or hypotheses formed by the researchers. From a social science point of view, this is good, reliable information. But precise answers to researchers' questions are unlikely to be of much use to teachers. And general principles and average trends are as likely to misinform as to inform a particular classroom teacher dealing with a particular child or group.

So, in terms of information, the vast bulk of the research literature will be of little practical use to any particular teacher. This is not to say that such research should be stopped. Rather, we should treat the research literature on, say, literacy, as a kind of encyclopedia that we consult for information as we need it, with our own local and specific questions in mind, and with a clear sense of the applicability of that information to our particular situation.

Inspiration

A second way in which research can serve thoughtful teachers is to provide inspiration. By inspiration I mean a picture of how schooling could be different, could be better, could become the world we imagined when we first signed on to become teachers. As the literacy critic and historian Walter Pater wrote 100 years ago: 'We need some imaginative stimulus, some not impossible ideal such as may shape vague hope, and transform it into effective desire, to carry us year after year, without disgust, through the routine-work which is so large a part of life' (Pater, 1907). I certainly need such a guiding pillar of cloud by day and pillar of fire by night to get me through the school year, and I think that research is one partial source of such inspiration.

My favourite example of an inspiring bit of research is the book *In the Early World* by Elwyn S. Richardson. It was published in 1964 as Educational Research Series No. 42 by the New Zealand Council of Educational Research, so it certainly qualifies as research. *In the Early World* is about learning to become literate in poetry, science, art and community building in a two-room country school in New Zealand. The report spans a five-year period of life at Oruaiti School and is rich with the words and artifacts produced by the children and the stories behind the artifacts. *In the Early World* is the most vivid example of complete integration of learning with life, art with science, and adults with children that I have ever read.

50

Now, the point of this example is not to urge you to recreate or to imitate the Oruaiti School of a generation ago. No, the inspiration for me comes from knowing and being able to visualize a time and place in which, with simple materials, ordinary children, and a bit of imagination and risk-taking, one teacher was able to foster the kinds of integrated learning experience that I value. Knowing that it is possible, knowing that it *did* happen, seeing the beautiful evidence in the haiku from which the book borrows its title, all of these help me to search for that extra spark, that constructive riskiness in my own teaching.

> *The blue heron stands in the early world,*
> *Looking like a freezing blue cloud in the morning.*
>   Irene

Vision

Research can broaden and sharpen our vision of the world of schooling by offering us concepts, models, and theories through which we can see our familiar surroundings in new ways. I believe that teacher boredom and burnout result, in part, from the feeling that one is trapped in a thoroughly predictable situation that is unlikely to change. But, even in such situations, it is possible to 'see' the situation differently, with the help of an outsider's point of view. When anthropologists work in their own culture, as when ethnographers of education study school classrooms, one of their biggest challenges is to 'make the familiar strange', to see with new eyes what they have learned to take for granted. When research provides tools for seeing the familiar setting of the classroom in new ways, researchers are indeed serving practice.

An example of research in the service of vision comes from my work with Susan Florio-Ruane on school writing. One analysis of a year-long descriptive study of the teaching of writing in elementary and middle school involved categorizing writing assignments on the basis of their forms and functions (Florio and Clark, 1982). Each of the major occasions for writing observed were sorted into one of four function categories: (1) writing to participate in community, (2) writing to know oneself and others, (3) writing to occupy free time and (4) writing to demonstrate academic competence. And each function category was described in terms of its initiator, composer, writer, audience, format, fate and evaluation. The importance of this example is not that our analysis is elegant, logical and supported by data, or that the study was published in *Research in the Teaching of English*. No, its importance lies in the fact that this descriptive framework helped at least one teacher to see and think about his own classroom differently as an environment for writing. He used the form and function categories from our research to examine the opportunities that his own students had to write, to plan for changes in his curriculum, and to ask more penetrating questions about writing activity ideas that came his way. In short, this teacher used research to come to a new vision of what his teaching was and could be.

Support

Finally, research can serve practising teachers by providing them with support for what they are already doing well. All too often, in my opinion, research in education is seen exclusively as a force for change. Usually, a call for change implies that what has gone before is faulty, inefficient, or inadequate to the task. Yet we know that, in many respects, North American and British schools are among the best in the world, and that truly terrible, damaging and incompetent teaching is rare.

At the same time, teaching is a solitary and potentially lonely profession in which individual teachers rarely have the time or opportunity to learn about and discuss how their own teaching compares with others. While research reports are certainly not a substitute for professional dialogue among teachers, research on teaching can provide both evidence for and explanations of why good teaching works as it does.

In this connection, I think of an example from research on teacher planning. A number of studies of planning for teaching (reviewed in Clark and Peterson, 1986) confirm that experienced teachers do not follow the so-called 'rational model' of planning typically prescribed in teacher education programmes (i.e., define learning objectives, generate alternatives, choose the optimum alternative, teach and evaluate). Rather, teachers typically start with an idea for a learning activity, which they elaborate and adapt to their own classroom situations. Further, this research describes elaborate interconnections among different levels of teacher planning (e.g., yearly, term, unit, weekly and daily planning). This line of research can be taken as supportive of teachers in at least two ways. First, it offers support for those teachers who do their planning in ways that are apparently adaptive to the complexity and constraints of the real classroom, but who might also feel guilty for not following the model that they were trained to use. Second, this research is a step towards acknowledging some of the invisible and unappreciated demands of the teaching profession and towards describing aspects of teaching that are truly professional and in the sense that the work of designers, physicians and lawyers is professional.

So, when I say, 'Let's demand service!', what I am calling for is a combination of information, inspiration, vision and support. Part of the responsibility for serving teachers rests with researchers; in the ways that they design their studies, share what they have learned, and call on practising teachers to cooperate in the process. And part of the responsibility lies with teachers, who can begin to seek and also call for more relevant information, as well as inspiration, vision and support from the research community.

LET'S GET CREATIVE!

When I call for more creativity I mean finding better ways to use the resources already available in the service of thoughtful teaching. I am reminded of the brother of a neighbour of mine who worked for Libby Foods. For years he saw Libby discarding tons and tons of pumpkin seeds as a waste product of the processing of pie filling. After much stove-top experimentation he invented a snack food of processed pumpkin seeds that is now being marketed nationally. I'd like to apply that same kind of creativity to the research literature that we already have on the shelf to try to realize more of the potential currently wasted.

Briefly, I propose that there are six different but related kinds of products of research on teaching that can be used to enrich the practice of teaching. The six classes of research outcomes are: 1) observed relationships among variables, 2) concepts, 3) theoretical models, 4) questions, 5) methods of inquiry and 6) case studies. I hope that by thinking more broadly and divergently about what research on teaching has to offer we might improve both the research and the practise of teaching as well. At the very least, both communities may come to believe that the grounds on which they could meet are larger in area and more varied and interesting in terrain than is typically thought.

Observed Relationships Among Variables

Classically, the fruits of the research process are expressed as 'findings and implications'. The 'findings' consist of brief summary descriptions of the observed relationships among variables studied, while the 'implications' are inferences drawn by the researchers that typically go beyond the data. To oversimplify, findings are observed facts about the world and implications are what the investigator believes these facts suggest about how practitioners should behave in situations similar to the ones studied. The facts that many researchers on teaching pursue consist of causal statements about the relationship between particular teacher behaviours and measured student achievement. Still other kinds of facts about teaching have been documented by researchers on teacher thinking who describe how teachers plan, process information, and make decisions (see Clark and Peterson, 1986). Both behaviourally- and cognitively-oriented research have played important roles in establishing research on teaching as a distinct and even thriving field, but the direct translation of findings and implications into prescriptions for teaching and teacher education has not worked well, for all of the reasons articulated by Cronbach (1975), Fenstermacher (1979), Phillips (1980), Floden and Feiman (1981) and Eisner (1984). In my judgement, the findings of research on teaching that describe observed relationships among teacher and student visible or cognitive behaviours are the least likely to be directly useful in the classroom.

However, I do have a suggestion that might yield additional mileage from re-examination of this research. I have long believed that ineffective teaching – poor teaching, if you will – is due less to the absence of particular effective strategies and teacher behaviours than it is a consequence of the *presence* of things that teachers sometimes do that sabotage what could otherwise be good teaching. When, for example, students are faced with double binds and mixed messages about competition and cooperation, meritocracy and egalitarianism, equality of opportunity and self-fulfilling prophecies about the normal distribution of achievement, even technically excellent teaching may have mediocre effects. What I propose is to rephrase the big question of researchers on teaching effectiveness from 'What kind of teaching works best in almost all situations?' (a discouraging question to pursue) to 'What have some teachers done sometimes that have fouled things up?' Taking this perspective, could a re-examination of the literature of research on teaching yield up ideas about what some of these avoidable impediments to good teaching and school learning are? And would it not make sense to include attention to these empirically observed impediments and pitfalls in our teacher preparation and professional development programmes? Remember that the Ten Commandments have stood up for so long, in part, because they constitute a short list largely about what we should *not* do, rather than a detailed prescription for what we should do. Perhaps *pro*scriptions are more easily generalized than *pre*scriptions.

The researchers who did the original work may have to be the ones who lead the search for evidence of impediments to good teaching, because explicit attention is seldom given to this side of teaching effectiveness when a study is first reported. Such evidence is more often present in the parts of the story that are left out of journal articles and technical reports or in sometimes speculative explanations of surprising or seemingly paradoxical findings. To illustrate from my own work, I was part of a team that did a laboratory study of teacher planning and teaching effectiveness (Peterson, Marx and Clark, 1978). One of our surprising findings was that, among 12 teachers who thought aloud while planning, there was a significant negative correlation between the number of planning statements they made and their students' post-teaching achievement scores. Paradoxically, more planning was associated with lower achievement, and that is where we left matters in 1978. Now, with years of hindsight, I have a more satisfying and logical explanation for this anomaly: the teachers with the largest numbers of planning statements were those who focused their attention almost exclusively on reading and reviewing content to be taught, giving little or no planning time to the process of instruction. These teachers legitimately used their planning time as a study and curriculum review session, and emerged with increased knowledge of their subject matter, but without a well thought-out plan for instruction. This leads me to make a practical suggestion: that teachers and prospective teachers should pay attention to how they spend their planning time, and what the balance is between attention to subject matter and attention to instructional process. Novices, especially, should be cautioned that planning for teaching is different from studying for a test, even though there is sometimes a test-like quality to observed sessions of student teaching.

Concepts

A second category of outcomes of research on teaching is concepts. By concepts I mean verbal labels for phenomena that researchers have found useful in describing the dynamics of the classroom, aspects of teaching and school learning, and the curriculum. From the researchers' point of view, concepts about teaching are seen as a means to the end of defining variables and subsequently measuring strength and direction of relationships among those variables. But I claim that concepts themselves, when they are usefully descriptive of teaching, are valuable products of research on teaching. Examples of concepts of this kind include academic learning time (Fisher, Berliner, Filby, Marliave, Cahen and Dishaw, 1980), academic work (Doyle, 1983), wait time (Rowe, 1974), the steering group (Lundgren, 1972), 'with-it-ness' (Kounin, 1970), incremental planning (Clark and Yinger, 1979), pedagogical content knowledge (Shulman, 1987), and the occasion for writing (Clark and Florio, *et al*. 1982). There are many more concepts of this kind that originated in research on teaching, that are not obvious to the naive observer of the practice of teaching, and that should be a part of the conceptual vocabulary of teachers. Concepts help us to organize, make sense of, communicate about and reflect on our experiences. A teacher education or professional development programme that equips its graduates with some of the means to make meaning, communicate and reflect is on the right track.

Theoretical Models

A third kind of product of research on teaching with potential practical application is the theoretical model. By this I mean verbal or graphic representations of the relationships among concepts in teaching–learning situations. Theoretical models can serve all of the functions that I attributed to concepts above, and they also provide a more comprehensive and dynamic framework for thinking about and perceiving classrooms in their complexity. Examples of theoretical models and constructs that could serve these purposes include the Carroll Model of School Learning (Carroll, 1963), Shavelson and Stern's (1981), and Peterson and Clark's (1978) models of teacher interactive decision-making, Yinger's (1977) process model of teacher planning, and the participation structure model of the classroom (Philips, 1972; Shultz, Florio and Erickson, 1982). It is important, I believe, that abstractions of the kind that these models represent be taken as heuristic and suggestive rather than as prescriptions for 'the correct way to think about teaching'. Indeed, their principal value to educators may be that exposure to multiple theoretical models could encourage teachers to examine, make explicit and refine their own implicit theories.

Questions

The fourth product of research on teaching on my list is questions. Here I commend to you both questions that are posed at the outset of a study and used to guide inquiry (typically called 'research questions') and also questions raised later when researchers are trying to make sense of the data and when calling for additional research. A teacher can learn a great deal about what is problematic in teaching by learning what challenging and partially answered questions thoughtful researchers are asking. Even (or perhaps especially) when questions seem to have no definitive answer they can serve to orient professional reflection. Similarly, researchers could learn a great deal from taking the concerns and dilemmas of practising teachers into account as they frame the questions that guide their research. Examples of generative questions that are being addressed by researchers on teaching include: Why is writing to difficult to teach? What are the possibilities and limitations of small group cooperative learning? What makes some schools more effective than others? What roles do textbooks play in school learning? How can individual differences in student aptitudes for learning be accommodated? What roles do teacher planning, judgement, and decision-making play in classroom instruction? How do teachers' implicit theories affect their perceptions and behaviour? What does it take to begin and sustain authentic educative conversations among schoolchildren?

Methods of Inquiry

Fifth, research on teaching can be a source of methods of inquiry. Researchers have invented and established the limitations of many techniques and tools for describing and understanding teaching. Teacher educators and teachers need ways of seeing, describing, and analysing the complexities of teaching that go beyond what one can do with unstructured live observations. Researchers have developed many category systems for counting and rating the quality of teacher-student interaction (Simon and Boyer, 1970), including some that focus on dyadic interaction between the teacher and particular students (e.g. Brophy and Good, 1974). The technology of micro-teaching was originally developed to meet the needs of researchers on teaching and has been adopted as a useful part of many teacher training programmes. More recently, researchers studying teachers' thought processes have employed stimulated recall, think aloud procedures, and structured journal writing to make visible the formerly hidden world of teaching. And practitioners of the ethnography of classrooms have provided us with clear examples of what their descriptive fieldwork methods can accomplish as well as improved guidelines for how to pursue this kind of inquiry and what some of its limitations are. All of these methods of inquiry offer interesting possibilities for adaptation in teacher preparation and professional development programmes if an important goal of continuing education is to equip teachers to be reflective, analytic and constructively critical of their own teaching.

Case Studies

Sixth, and finally, research on teaching has recently been producing case studies – rich and thick descriptions of classroom events ranging in duration from a few moments to an entire school year. Case studies can serve a number of valuable purposes for teachers, including illustration of concepts and theoretical models in context, providing opportunities to analyse and reflect on real classroom events from a variety of disciplinary points of view, and illustrating how the perspective held by the researcher shapes and limits the form and content of the resulting case study. My colleagues Robert Floden, Susan Florio-Ruane and I began using case studies from research on teaching in the early 1980s to serve these purposes in undergraduate and graduate education courses in educational psychology, the philosophy of education, and language arts methods. Since then, written cases and shorter vignettes have become increasingly available in collections derived from research studies[1] or specially written for use in teacher education curriculum.[2] The fourth and fifth cases printed in Part Three of this book were first written in conjunction with descriptive research projects, and subsequently adapted for use in teacher education and professional development.

The Promise of Creative Thinking

Research on teaching has a great deal to offer to teachers in real classrooms if we think more broadly about what research actually produces. Observed relationships among operationally defined variables in a particular study may be the primary product of research for the audience of other researchers. But teachers can help themselves develop as reflective and autonomous professionals by thinking from the concepts, models, questions, methods of inquiry, and case studies that research on teaching also produces. The teacher, so prepared, still faces a complex and demanding problem solving situation in his or her own classroom, and research on teaching probably will not make the process of teaching simpler. But creative use of the unexploited outcomes of research on teaching can make teaching more appropriately complex.

LET'S GET COMMUNICATING!

My fourth and final exhortation, 'Let's get communicating!', concerns the discourse between researchers and teachers and among teachers themselves.

Neither teachers nor researchers are very adept at professional communication about professional matters. I suspect that none of us is fully satisfied by the traditional media of journal articles, textbooks, half-day in-service workshops, or evening and summer courses at the local teachers' college. Even when done well, these traditional approaches to professional communication fall short of genuine service to teachers.

For a period of six years my colleagues and I worked to develop a new setting for professional communication called the Written Literacy Forum. The Forum was a collaborative effort by teachers and researchers to develop more thoughtful connections between literacy researchers and teachers. Founded in September 1981, the Forum conducted inquiry into the relationship between written literacy research and the teaching of writing through two kinds of activity: (1) Forum deliberations, in which the nine members (five teachers and four researchers) discussed and analysed key issues in the teaching of writing, and (2) planning, delivery and reflection on in-service workshops on writing instruction. In both of these major activities we drew from the substantial data base (Clark and Florio, *et al.*, 1982) collected in the Michigan State University Written Literacy Project, in which all initial Forum members were participants, from the research literature on writing instruction, and from the extensive practical experiences of the teachers and researchers themselves. By these means we sought to develop thoroughly grounded and practical ways of bringing the fruits of research on writing into action in the classroom.

The Written Literacy Forum was created as one possible answer to the challenge of bringing research and practice together. In creating it we modified the traditional culture of research that defines teachers as 'subjects', researchers as 'data analysts', and teacher-educators as 'change agents'. Each participant in the Written Literacy Forum took on all of these roles and more. New social, methodological and theoretical forms developed as we talked, planned and told stories about teaching and learning of writing in schools. The Forum extended the conventional boundaries of teaching, research, and teacher education. In a positive social atmosphere trust and dialogue arose, deep friendships and personal connections developed, yielding increased knowledge about the process of writing instruction, and insight into the process of professional development as experienced by practitioners and researchers alike.

One example of the influence of Forum deliberations on our research agenda evolved from discussions by Forum teachers of the practical problem of when and how to provide constructive feedback to children during the composition process. How do you help a young writer without discouraging? This issue was a real problem for teachers of the primary grades through graduate school. Serious cases were contrasted with situations in which providing constructive feedback was not so problematic. These discussions, and the insights and questions that they stimulated, led us to realize that this is as much a human relations problem as it is a technical issue, and that it will continue to be problematic, in the sense that no single prescribed solution will work in every case. All of us understand the problem better, while at the same time recognizing that we must each address it in the unique contexts of our own classrooms. Most importantly, we all realize that providing constructive, responsive feedback is *intrinsically* difficult, rather than difficult only for the incompetent teacher.

Forum deliberations also influenced the ways we taught. One example involves a primary teacher and Forum member who reports that she dramatically increased the number of opportunities for her students to do writing for audiences other than herself. She attributed her decision to promote writing for audiences outside the classroom to her participation in Forum discussions of two issues: the fundamental function of writing as a medium that can bridge time and distance, and the importance of writing activities feeling meaningful and consequential to authors. (Our earlier research on written literacy indicated that activities that seemed to students to have no purpose beyond pleasing the teacher were difficult to manage and rarely produced good writing.) The importance of this change in a teacher's practice lies not in the particulars of how she teaches differently. Rather, it is more significant that she has internalized a new question to pursue as she refines her own curriculum: How can I make this activity more meaningful and consequential for the children?

My experience of the six years of the Written Literacy Forum suggests that professional communication can be raised to new levels of usefulness when we invest the time and energy it takes to make it happen. Writing was a good choice of focus for our deliberations because it is a richly problematic part of the curriculum. But I see no reason why the Forum concept would not work equally well if the focus were other than writing. In fact, teacher–researcher collaborative groups have begun to spring up in support of women teaching science (Cavazos, 1994), teaching mathematics for understanding (Featherstone *et al.*, 1992), primary school teaching (McConaghy, 1991), and promoting critical democracy in teaching (Swidler, 1994). The general point holds: bringing the fruits of research into practice seems to require an intermediate step in which intelligent practitioners, through deliberation, make the important connections and adaptations themselves. As a researcher I may be able to facilitate this process a bit, but I certainly can't expect to force 'my models' on unwilling teachers. Face-to-face communication among teachers and between teachers and researchers is crucial to bringing research into practice.

CONCLUSION

In conclusion, teachers and researchers must cooperate if research on teaching is to be of real service to teaching. We need to get humble, to demand service, to get creative, and to communicate. Pursuing these four exhortations will look quite different in different professional settings. But, unless we all take care to pursue each of them, research and practice will continue to go their separate ways.

NOTES

*This chapter was first published as 'Research into practice: cautions and qualifications' in *The Contexts of School-Based Literacy*, edited by T. Raphael (Random House, 1984) and is reprinted with the permission of McGraw-Hill, Inc.

1 Kleinfeld, J. S. (1990) *Teaching cases in cross-cultural education*. Fairbanks: University of Alaska, Department of Education, Publications Center. Rowland, S. (1984) *The Enquiring Classroom*. New York: Falmer.

2 Greenwood, G. E. and Parkay, F. (1989) *Case studies for teacher decision-making*. New York: Random House. Kauffman, J. M., Mostert, M. P., Nuttycombe, D. G., Trent, S. C. and Hallahan, D. P. (1993) *Managing classroom behavior: A reflective-case-based approach*. Boston: Allyn & Bacon. Silvereman, R., Welty, W. M. and Lyon, S. (1992) *Case studies for teacher problem solving*. New York: McGraw-Hill.

Chapter 6

Real Lessons from Imaginary Teachers

> There is no steady unretracing progress in this life; we do not
> advance through fixed gradation, and at the last one pause:
> through infancy's unconscious spell, boyhood's thoughtless faith,
> adolescent's doubt (the common doom), then skepticism, then
> disbelief, resting at last in manhood's pondering repose of If. But
> once gone through, we trace the round again; and are infants,
> boys, and men, and Ifs eternally. Where lies the final harbor,
> whence we unmoor no more?

> Herman Melville, *Moby Dick*

This story developed from a series of rare and happy coincidences. A woman
named Susan Hall had taught English in a Northern California secondary school
for 20 years. She agreed to become the subject of a qualitative research project.
One year later, unbeknown to the first researcher, she agreed (somewhat reluctantly) to participate in a second qualitative study of her teaching. The two
researchers did their work, and eventually published case descriptions of Susan
Hall, masking her identity with two different pseudonyms.

I met Susan Hall in June 1988 when she, again reluctantly, agreed to
participate in a two-week workshop on advanced supervision that I co-directed at
Stanford University. By this time Susan Hall was getting ready to come in from
the cold: she revealed to me and to the other workshop participants that she was
also known as 'Nancy' in the *Harvard Educational Review* article (Shulman,
1987) that happened to be on the workshop reading list. (The vignette describing
Nancy came from the doctoral dissertation of Sigrun Gudmundsdottir, 1989.) As
luck would have it, Grace Grant was a guest presenter at the workshop, on her
second day as director of the Stanford Secondary Teacher Education Program.
Grace Grant was the other researcher who had become a student of Susan Hall's
teaching.

As they say in the movies, time passed. My next contact with Susan Hall and
Grace Grant was in June 1989 when Susan was now co-leading the advanced
supervision workshop with me and Grace was again a guest presenter. Near the
end of my visit to California, Grace invited me to take part in a symposium where

she, Sigrun Gudmundsdottir and Susan Hall would each tell their sides of the story. I agreed with enthusiasm.

The intellectual problem that I set for myself was to think hard about what lessons and ideas about teaching and research could be drawn from the unusual experiences of Susan Hall, Grace Grant and Sigrun Gudmundsdottir. Months of thinking, writing and revision led me to condense my lessons learned into three topics. The first is reflected in the title 'Real lessons from imaginary teachers', and deals with developmental and situational dynamics in teaching. Second, I explore how researchers' intentions and expectations frame and focus what we see. And, third, I was moved to think and write about how what begins as a simple description of teaching often becomes intervention into teacher thought and action.

IMAGINARY TEACHERS, REAL LESSONS, AND CHANGE OVER TIME

Every Armenian folktale begins with the same words: 'A long, long time ago there *was* and *was not* . . . ' One of the meanings of this paradoxical expression is that there is at the same time truth and fiction in what follows; that even the most extraordinary and improbably exaggerated tales can be vessels for enduring and reliable truths about human nature and the world. This, too, is the meaning of the title: 'Real lessons from imaginary teachers'.

Now, Susan Hall is not imaginary. She is a real person. But what *we* have to work with and to think from are *images* of Susan Hall, at different times, under different circumstances, and portrayed by different storytellers pursuing different agendas. The images of Susan Hall, and of other teachers depicted in research literature, are fixed in words, pictures and numbers. But these images don't give us complete or contemporary representations of the real teachers, the real people, as they live and work and think today. The literature of educational research is peopled with imaginary teachers, frozen in time.

Consider some of the teachers who have worked with me in research projects during the last 15 years. One left teaching to become a New York stockbroker, then moved to New Orleans. Her second graders (7-year-olds) of 1978 are now college students. Some of these teachers have moved to different classes, schools or communities. One became a reading helping teacher and founded her own repertory company. Another has retired. Their images remain fixed in print, in memory, while their lives are quite dynamic. Real lessons from imaginary teachers.

THE FIRST IMAGE OF SUSAN

Grace Grant convinced Susan Hall to allow her to become a non-participant observer in her 12th grade (17-year-old) Advanced Placement[1] English literature class for two weeks in 1984. Grace had been an English teacher colleague of

Susan's 15 years earlier and had later become a researcher and teacher educator, while Susan ' ... continued to refine a teaching expertise and passion for literature that I (Grace) admired and respected' (Grant, 1991, p. 405). Grace's agenda was to write a book describing how four teachers promoted reasoning and critical thinking among their students.

Grace visited and observed the 12th grade (17-year-old) class for eight hours during the two weeks of fieldwork, and interviewed Susan once at the beginning of the study (focusing on Susan's subject matter knowledge and goals for students) and once at the end (focusing on transformations of subject matter in teaching reasoning). These interview topics were selected and framed by Grace, rather than allowed to develop serendipitously in conversation. In addition to field notes and interview transcripts, Grace copied course descriptions, handouts and assignment specifications. Drawing on these data later, Grace created an image of Susan's teaching literature as, metaphorically, like climbing Mt Everest (an image that Susan had used in class to describe the challenge and the thrill of mastering a difficult piece of literature). Susan was portrayed as the leader of this alpine expedition, experienced at high altitude trekking, guiding, encouraging, warning and questioning her charges along the way. The two particular literary works being addressed during the study were Faulkner's short story *The Bear* and Shakespeare's *King Lear*.

In addition to the surface story of how Susan used questions, written assignments and tests to make her students more thoughtful and attentive to detail about literature, a second story played out between these the two women. It was a story of caution, defensiveness and mutual misunderstanding, mostly attributed by Grace to her reserved, shy, one-sided way of relating to Susan. What Grace intended as 'not interfering' was felt by Susan as 'holding back'. What Grace intended as consideration for the teacher's busy schedule, Susan saw as disinterest. When Grace shared a draft description of the final day of class before spring break (intended to show how a teacher brings closure to a complex unit), Susan reacted angrily, believing that this most rushed and unrepresentative day was to stand for what was typical of her teaching. Eventually, the relational breach was healed, and the two continued to work together. But the breakdown illustrates how important relational issues are, and how at odds two interpretations of the same events can be, even by people who share the same culture and background.

THE SECOND IMAGE OF SUSAN

During a four-month period in 1985, Sigrun Gudmundsdottir interviewed Susan five times and observed and recorded her teaching of an American literature class 20 times. The research approach was qualitative in that Sigrun set out to describe and understand the perspectives and systems of rules underlying Susan's teaching. Sigrun chose to study Susan because her principal (head teacher) nominated her as an experienced teacher with a deep knowledge of English literature, and also because Susan voluntarily agreed to participate in the research (although, when first approached, Susan declined to participate, recalling her discomfort in the Grace Grant study). Susan was one of four teachers studied, all volunteers and each called 'experienced'. In Sigrun's words, 'Like her colleagues she was an excellent informant. She was reflective, articulate, expressive, and enjoyed her participation in the study' (Gudmundsdottir, 1991, p. 412).

Five interviews and 20 classroom observations yielded hundreds of pages of transcript and field notes. These, along with videotapes and memories, were the data from which Sigrun distilled a story and constructed an image of Susan Hall's teaching manner, philosophy and beliefs as an English teacher. Sigrun's interpretation of the data was constrained by her inexperience as a researcher (this was her doctoral dissertation), by her knowledge that Susan was nominated as an excellent and knowledgeable teacher, and by the need to learn something of relevance to the funded research project's agenda of which Sigrun's study was a part. The topic of the funded research project was teachers' subject matter knowledge and their representation of it.

What did Sigrun Gudmundsdottir learn from studying Susan Hall? Not surprisingly, she portrayed Susan as an excellent teacher with a deep and sophisticated knowledge of the literature that she teaches. In their first interview, Susan described a four-level model of literature comprehension, ranging from literal understanding of a text, through connotative meaning, interpretation, to the highest level: application of literature to one's own life. As Sigrun observed and took notes, Susan's articulated model seemed to be an accurate answer to the anthropologist's question, 'What is going on here?' In other words, it seemed that the teacher had done the work of the researcher, telling her in advance what to 'see'.

After close analysis of her classroom observation data, however, Sigrun concluded that the model in practice was different from the model in theory. In practice, Susan's teaching could best be described by a three-part model, dropping the 'connotative meaning' category. More significantly, Susan was portrayed as working primarily on having her students become proficient at interpretation of literary symbolism in the texts, and very rarely on application to their own lives.

The second image of Susan, then, is of a highly competent teacher who knows her material, who has articulated a sophisticated hierarchical model of learning aims culminating in connecting literature to her students' lives, but whose day-to-day practice dwells much more on practising traditional scholastic skills of recognizing classical literary devices and interpreting the author's imagery. The lesson that Susan taught Sigrun was more methodological than substantive. As Sigrun wrote later, 'It is a serious interpretive mistake in qualitative research when the teacher's story becomes the researcher's story and the researcher does not know it' (Gudmundsdottir, 1991, p. 413).

SUSAN'S REFLECTIONS ON HER TWO IMAGES

' ... when I reread your published studies what struck me was how accurately you both captured me, but in two different settings, with different age and ability levels of the students, in two different years, using two different research methods. I was your "Linda", and I was Sigrun's "Nancy". But these descriptions were embedded in two very different classes under very different circumstances' (Hall and Grant, 1991, p. 425). In hindsight, Susan Hall recognizes herself in the two descriptions written by Grace Grant and Sigrun Gudmundsdottir. But she also sees the differences, and would not be surprised if a naive reader did not realize that the teacher called 'Linda' and the teacher called 'Nancy' are the same person. In fact, she suggests that they are *not* the same person, because who she is with her students is a circumstantial, responsive, relational matter. 'The teacher changes instructional techniques continually to meet the ever-changing needs of the group. Today I'm not even the exact same teacher in three sections of the same class. This year I have three senior (17-year-olds) AP (Advanced Placement) English classes, and someone can come in to watch all three and not see me teach the lesson in the same way three hours in a row because of what happens in that dynamic classroom interaction' (Hall and Grant, 1991, p. 425).

DEVELOPMENTAL DYNAMICS IN TEACHING

One of the strong messages of research on teacher thinking is about the complexities of teaching. Studies of teacher planning and decision-making illustrated two facets of complexity in teaching: that much of what a teacher must deal with is uncertain or unpredictable, and that there is too much going on in a classroom at any one time to attend to everything. The Susan Hall studies cause me to think about another facet of the complexity of teaching, namely, that teachers change over time. Teachers change developmentally and these changes are not limited to the first months and years of teaching. Attending to the developmental dynamics of teaching raises some interesting questions about the classical idea of reliability or stability of teacher behaviour and its effects.

Most researchers on teaching are concerned with discovering and documenting causes, effects and processes that are stable over time and that might generalize to new situations. This proclivity is built into the logic of the scientific method and the hopes of applied inquiry in education. But this special chance to think about a twice-studied teacher has shifted my attention from that which is stable and common in Susan's teaching to that which is dynamic and evolving.

In these studies of Susan Hall I see an analogue of Monet's series paintings of 100 years ago. The Impressionists' commitment to immediacy and the transience of a crystal moment is most dramatically alive in Monet's multiple renderings of grain stacks, river views, and garden scenes. Within each of these series, the subject is recognizably constant. But it is *the differences* in light and shadow, in warmth and tone, in texture and colour, that move us and educate our vision.

Or consider a personal example of developmental and situational human change: the case of Daniel Vincent Clark (one of my sons). Figure 6.1 consists of 12 school portraits of Daniel, beginning with kindergarten and ending with his secondary school yearbook photograph. When displayed side-by-side like this, each photo is clearly of Daniel. Yet what is most striking, I think, is what happens *between* successive photos – the developmental changes that we can infer from the apparently different Daniels who appear for the annual portrait sitting. (For those interested in solving a little puzzle, there is one photo missing. Which school year is *not* represented here?)

Now look at Figure 6.2. This collage also has Daniel Vincent Clark as its subject. All of these photographs were taken during his 18th year. The marked differences among these representations of Daniel reflect multiple facets of his personality brought out by situational differences. The student, the clown, the musician, the gardener, the waiter, the philosopher, the affectionate little boy, the big brother, the model – all crowd the page claiming to be the real Daniel. And each claim is valid. Daniel was all of these and more that year.

My point in all of this is that Susan Hall was and is just as complex and multifaceted as Dan Clark. And this is true of every teacher we study. Perhaps what was done accidentally here – to do two successive qualitative studies of one teacher – ought to be done intentionally and often in the future. Thereby we could begin to build our knowledge of the developmental and situational dynamics of expertise in thoughtful teaching.

FRAMING AND FOCUSING BY RESEARCHERS

A few summers ago I saw a film that I enjoyed immensely. The setting was a private residential school for boys. Although I have never met any of the actors, I left the theatre feeling that I knew some of them pretty well – I knew what they believed about teaching, about discipline, about English literature and poetry, about duty, honour, despair, growing up, and about the meaning of life. We had spent but two hours together, eavesdropping on private and public conversations, me not saying a word, not asking a direct question of my own. Yet I could predict how they would act and react in new situations, and I did successfully predict some of the turns of the cinematic story as it unfolded. (The film was called *Dead Poets Society* in the USA and *Carpe Diem* elsewhere.)

I left the theatre newly confirmed in some of my own beliefs about schooling: that teaching can be risky business; that the heart of good teaching is getting something insatiable started in the minds and hearts of others and then getting out of the way; that poetry is a most volatile gift; that growing up and growing old

Figure 6.1   Images of Daniel, aged 5 to 17

Figure 6.2   Images of Daniel's eighteenth year

make intrinsically painful, bittersweet and funny drama; that education is profoundly moral business.

My question here is: What was this film about? About teaching? About learning? Adolescent development? The pedagogical content knowledge of a teacher of English? About organizational development? The persistence of institutions, their norms and values? About the subtleties of child abuse in the families of the wealthy? About the ways of élitism, love and death?

An easy but unhelpful answer is that the film was about all of these things. But what was it primarily about? What was the central theme, the telling story? I claim that the answer to these questions depends as much on the viewer as on the intentions of the filmmaker. The viewer's alertness, background experience, ideology, company and reasons for seeing the film all have an influence on the sense that he or she makes of it. The experience of seeing this film may evoke rather different meanings, understandings and emotional reactions for different moviegoers. Seeing a film a second time or reading a book twice produces different understandings in the mind of a single observer. And two viewers seeing two different films starring the same actor would likely produce two rather different accounts of who that actor is, of what she can do well, of her strengths and limitations in relation to two different scripts and casts.

Now I want to connect all this with issues that arise in qualitative research on teaching, and specifically with the two studies of Susan Hall's teaching. First, we have Susan Hall, a good teacher and a dynamic, developing professional. She is not quite the same person today as she was yesterday. In my company she has had chances to play different roles and make different moves than she has in the company of 29 California adolescents. And we have Grace Grant, a researcher and teacher educator interested in critical thinking and how it is cultivated (Grant, 1988). And Sigrun Gudmundsdottir, doing a doctoral dissertation as part of a project on teachers' pedagogical content knowledge and how it is transformed in interaction with secondary school students. We have two weeks of contact; four months of contact. We have colleagues and doctoral committee members helping with interpretation and expression. We have two different school years.

We should not be surprised by or alarmed about the differences in these two portrayals of Susan Hall. In fact, I propose that we stop thinking of this work as two studies of Susan Hall's teaching. Rather, what I think we have here is one study of teaching for critical thinking and another of pedagogical content knowledge in the teaching of English. These are constructs, offered and defined by the researchers, illustrated and brought alive in the behaviour of a human teacher, who happened to be Susan Hall. We have a record of Grace Grant's thinking, analysis and empirically grounded theorizing about teaching and learning. And a separate case of Sigrun Gudmundsdottir's thinking, analysis and grounded theorizing about a teacher's knowledge, thought and action. Reading these cases can tell us more about the wisdom and perspectives of the authors than about Susan Hall.

WHEN DESCRIPTION BECOMES INTERVENTION

Both of the research projects that Susan Hall agreed to participate in are instances of naturalistic descriptive inquiry. Each researcher asked, in one way or another, that Susan teach just as she does when no researcher is present. There were no experimental treatments or teacher training sessions or specifications of desirable ways to teach. The researcher came to see, to hear, to learn, but not to change. Like the signs I've seen in national parks, the descriptive researcher's motto seems to be 'Take only pictures, leave only footprints'.

My claim, however, is that naturalistic descriptive research on teaching *does* change things in the classrooms under study, and that such research can instigate changes that reverberate for months and even years. The footprints we leave and the pictures we take make a difference in the lives and work of teachers and students.

Becoming a teacher–participant in a study of one's own teaching promotes self-consciousness in a number of ways. When I am observed by an expert judge of good teaching, I want to look my best. I try harder than I otherwise might to be at the top of my form. If you ask about my plans before I teach, I am more explicit (and perhaps more planful) than usual. When you interview me after teaching, I try to be more analytic and insightful about what went on than I would be with only myself as audience. Watching videotapes of my teaching gives me a special view of myself, rarely seen and sometimes disconcerting. Reading a published report describing my teaching, my thinking, my classroom, changes the way I see and think about myself.

Participation in research of this kind calls for articulation of what you are doing and why, what you believe and love about content, students and context. It is unusual for teachers to have an intelligent, patient, interested audience for such reflections. It takes courage and confidence to take a stand that might be criticized. Teachers can discover what they believe by telling it to another. Or, in the language of research on teacher thinking, they make their implicit theories explicit. This, in turn, can affect how they teach and see and act subsequently.

Images, perspectives, insights and feelings come from opening up the private world of one's teaching to an informed outsider. And these words and pictures don't necessarily fade or stop coming when data collection ends. Yesterday's explanations can frame tomorrow's plans. Articulated beliefs and once implicit theories are now more available as guides and standards for teacher thought and action. Having your teaching portrayed in the pages of the *Harvard Educational Review*, even under a pseudonym, can change your life for a while.

Not every descriptive study changes teachers in all of these ways. But I offer these possibilities as food for thought by researchers and teachers alike. I believe that we can no longer ignore the fact that teacher collaboration in research brings changes with it, only some of which we typically attend to or take note of. We *do* affect the people with whom we work in these ways. Descriptive research is a form of clinical intervention for which not many researchers and teachers are well-prepared. With mutual care and courage, researchers and teachers can change for the better, learn real lessons, and become ever more thoughtful about classroom life.

At the end of a retrospective interview, years after Grace Grant's and Sigrun Gudmundsdottir's images of Susan Hall had been published and disseminated around the world, Grace asked Susan: 'Would you agree to participate in another classroom research project?' Susan replied: 'Yes, I would. People think it's crazy to volunteer to be someone's guinea pig for months on end. But it was an exciting experience. I learned a great deal about my teaching and my students. Having daily observations can be like having a mirror there constantly: this reflector provides the opportunity not only to see what I have done but also to talk about the act of teaching with someone in a way that doesn't happen in most school settings. It is very different in purpose and process from a typical teacher–evaluation visit, where the observer visits occasionally, briefly describes the performance and gives a few comments. Few teachers or administrators have the time for the extended observation that you and Sigrun provided, or are as skilled at the kind of anecdotal note-taking and questioning that fostered my thinking about my work. What happened in these projects is more like the best peer coaching than evaluation, giving me the chance to hear someone say, "As a teacher, you did these things. Let's talk about why you did them." It gives me a chance to analyse my own instructional techniques. It can be non-threatening and, in many ways, stimulating. Being an educational guinea pig has probably been one of the most exciting activities of my 26-year teaching career' (Hall and Grant, 1991, p. 427).

NOTE

1 Advanced placement classes are honours sections in which student performance is evaluated by a nationally available standardized test which, when passed with high marks, may be counted as university credits, resulting in 'advanced placement' in the first year at university.

PART THREE

PORTRAITS OF THOUGHTFUL TEACHING

One morning, far, far away, but closer than you think, all the teachers gathered on a high plateau that overlooked the rolling plain of earth, with its forests, deserts, rivers and cities. Then the teachers began speaking, one by one, telling the story of a life – everything seen, heard, and felt by each soul. As the voices dreamed and remembered, a vast, bluish mist enveloped the land and the seas below. Nothing was visible. It was as if the earth had evaporated. Now there was nothing but the voices and the stories and the mist; and the teachers were afraid to stop the storytelling and afraid not to stop, because no one knew where the earth had gone.

Finally, when only a few storytellers remained to take a turn, someone shouted: 'Stop! Enough, enough of this talk! Enough of us have spoken! We must find the earth again!'

Suddenly, the mist cleared. Below the teachers, the earth had changed. It had grown into the shape of the stories they'd told – a shape as wondrous and new and real as the words they'd spoken. But it was also a world unfinished, because not all of the stories had been told.

Some say that death and evil entered the world because some of the teachers had no chance to speak. Some say that the world would be worse than it is if all the stories had been told. Some say that there are no more stories to tell. Some believe that untold stories are the only ones of value and that we are lost when they are lost. Some are certain that the storytelling never stops; and this is one more story; and the earth always lies under its blanket of mist, being born.

(Adapted from 'Father Stories' by John Edgar Wideman, *The New Yorker*, 1 August 1994, p. 36)

How does a good teacher help us develop our appreciation of an abstract concept into a deep, real and practical understanding? One path to understanding is through examples, through cases and situated stories that show what ideas like colonialism, or justice, or care, or isomorphism look like in the flesh. The best teachers, in my experience, are the ones who offer the best examples. And the best teachers find themselves in career-long searches for apt and memorable illustrations of the ideas they want their students to master.

Section Three, Portraits of Thoughtful Teaching, offers five case studies of teaching, set variously in a university, a secondary school, and in a primary school. Each case is, at first glance, rather ordinary in circumstance. But, with a second look, we see that many everyday activities and dilemmas in the lives of teachers call for wise judgement, compassion, patience and principled action. In other words, opportunities for thoughtfulness in teaching arise often, perhaps daily, when we are alert for them.

I hope that this handful of cases will enrich your sense of the variety of meanings of thoughtful teaching and of situations that call for thoughtfulness. More importantly, I hope that you will begin to see and to tell stories of thoughtful teaching that arise from your own experiences. For the most vivid and telling examples are the ones that we construct for ourselves.

Chapter 7

Case One: Teaching William a Lesson

Honesty is an essential virtue for the survival and operation of any human organization. Most laws have to do with honesty. Dishonesty and deceptiveness are despised among the powerless and powerful alike. The school and the classroom could not operate without substantial honesty. And the guiding idea of the university is the pursuit of truth, which is the fundamental referent of honesty.

What is this virtue called honesty? The positive side of the definition concerns telling the truth and acting in ways wholly consistent with what you know or believe to be true. The negative side of the definition involves refraining from cheating, lying, representing the work of another as your own, stealing and other dishonest deeds. The temptation to dishonesty is almost always laced with self-interest, making it a particularly difficult virtue to practise for the young and the immature of any age.

Much of a teacher's concern with encouraging honesty among students has to do with telling the truth and preventing or correcting cheating. Consider this example from a textbook for teachers more than 100 years old:

> At Harrow, two boys brought me [Canon Farrar] exercises marked
> by the same grotesque mistakes. It seemed certain that those
> exercises could not have been done independently. Both boys
> assured me that there had been no copying. One whom I had
> considered a boy of high morale assured me of this again and
> again with passionate earnestness. I said to him, 'If I were to
> send up these two exercises to any jury in England, they would
> say that these resemblances could not be accidental, except by
> something almost like a miracle. But you both tell me that you
> have not copied. I cannot believe that you would lie to me. I must
> suppose that there has been some extraordinary accident. I shall
> say no more.' Years after, that boy, then a monitor, said to me:
> 'Sir, do you remember that exercise in the fourth form?' 'Yes', I
> said. 'Well, sir, I told you a lie. It was copied. You believed me, and
> the rememberance of that lie has remained with me and pained
> me ever since.' 'I am inclined to think', says Canon Farrar, 'that

> boy was more effectually taught and more effectually punished
> than if I had refused to accept his protests."[1]

Except for the dated language, this example might be used in the contemporary preparation of teachers. But look again. Canon Farrar resorted to dishonesty himself in the apparent belief that this would be the most effective and humane way to inculcate honesty in the two boys. Can we believe that the boys did not know at the time that he was lying, toying with them, laying a trap and levying a corrosive burden of guilt upon them? Canon Farrar fails us (and the Harrow boys) as a model of honest and courageous confrontation of cheating and lying. Dishonesty by the teacher, however well motivated, inspires cynicism, guilt, and resentment at hypocrisy, but not necessarily honesty. Morally flawed means promote morally damaging ends.

A contemporary case of a teacher's response to plagiarism gives us a more constructive model:

Dr Stevens wished that this was not happening to him. One of his under-graduates in a course on instructional design, a varsity football player but not a varsity scholar, had just turned in a written assignment that was manifestly not his own work. The topic of William's paper was appropriate for the assignment, but not one that he knew much about. The task analysis and the instructional design were sophisticated and complete. The use of written language was much more clear and forceful than any that William had heretofore demonstrated. But, most damning of all, Dr Stevens recognized this paper: it had been written by another student of this course, one year previously.

As Dr Stevens looked into the matter further, it became more of a mess. His records showed that George, the original author of the paper, had received a 'deferred' grade for the course – the final version of the paper had never reached the professor. A telephone call revealed that George had indeed deposited his final work in Dr Stevens' postbox, and that it must have been stolen. What Dr Stevens had remembered was reading and providing feedback on an earlier draft of this paper. Fortunately, George still had a copy of the draft, and he delivered it to Dr Stevens. As with Canon Farrar's case, any jury would see that the resemblances between William's and George's papers could not be accidental.

What to do, what to do? Dr Stevens called William and the Academic Advisor for the Athletic Department, told each what he had discovered, and arranged a meeting of the three. At the meeting, everyone was embarrassed. Dr Stevens laid out the evidence. William confessed to having had help but said that everyone he knew did this kind of thing and that, after all, he had changed some of the wording of George's original text. The Academic Advisor said 'flunk him'. That was a tempting and unequivocal way for the professor to terminate the problem.

Instead, Dr Stevens proposed that the Athletic Department hire one of his graduate students to work with William on the assignment in question during the next four weeks. William would be expected to select a new topic, analyse how he would teach this topic to another person, and design and write a detailed plan and programme of instruction. With this help, William did complete the assignment and passed the course. Today he is a professional football player.

What did William learn from this painful episode? In Dr Stevens' view, he learned: 1) that cheating doesn't work; 2) that there are legitimate ways to get help with challenging assignments; 3) that, with help, William had what it takes to do the work and learn the content of the course; and 4) that honest work takes about the same amount of effort as dishonest work, and you don't feel guilty afterwards. At a more fundamental level, William learned about respect and forgiveness. Dr Stevens expressed his moral responsibility to respect each of his students by taking the time and trouble to treat William as a responsible human being, to connect him with the tutorial help that he needed, and to provide detailed feedback on William's written work. Respect and forgiveness combined in Dr Stevens' clear refusal to join the lie (that the first paper was substantially William's work) or to act on the 'one mistake and you're dead' principle implicit in the Athletic Department Advisor's advice. For Dr Stevens, and for teachers generally, honesty, respect, compassion and forgiveness mean more work, not less. Morally responsible teaching requires that we go beyond, sometimes far beyond, the letter of the laws of technically effective teaching.

A final point about this confrontation of dishonesty by honesty: Dr Stevens solved his problem by reframing it in the form: 'How can I help William to do and learn the ideas and skills that are at the heart of this course?' Dr Stevens stayed with his morally grounded assumption and belief that all students can learn. By turning the moral, interpersonal, legal mess into a pedagogical problem that he thought he could solve, Dr Stevens both taught effectively and lived up to his moral responsibility.

NOTE

1   Allen J. (1887) *Mind Studies for young teachers*. New York: E. L. Kellogg and Co.

Chapter 8

Case Two: The Gatekeeper's Dilemma

One of the most difficult and painful moments for a teacher is the decision to fail a student. And for a teacher of teachers, the worst decision of all is the decision to fail a student teacher. Failing student teaching means that the student will not be certified as a teacher; will probably never achieve his or her goal of becoming a teacher. Since student teaching comes late in most teacher education programmes, the bad news comes after months or years of more or less successful performance – stopped just short of the prize. And failing a student teacher also declares a failure on the part of the teacher education faculty and of a cooperating teacher to help the student become an adequate beginning teacher. There is plenty of pain to be shared in this situation.

Nancy was the field supervisor to whom this decision fell. She has been a university field supervisor of student teachers for 11 years, and during the last six years has supervised pre-student teaching and student teaching field experiences in a selective 30- student elementary teacher preparation programme. This programme is one of five teacher education programmes in a large college of education from which approximately 750 certified teachers graduate each spring.

How did Nancy make the decision to fail her student, and how does she remember and explain these events in hindsight? What was difficult and painful about this situation, and what role did thoughtfulness play?

The story of Nancy and Jenine extends over more than a year. Jenine came to Nancy's attention as a student who was having problems in coursework by the middle of the first year of her programme. Jenine's attendance problems and attitude problems were severe enough during the spring of her first year that she was given an 'Incomplete' for the spring course. From Nancy's point of view, each bit of progress by Jenine in one area was offset by new problems arising. By the autumn term of Jenine's senior year, when she was in a pre-student teaching field placement, it became more and more clear to Nancy that Jenine could not handle even routine classroom demands. The programme goal of having Jenine take responsibility for the elementary classroom for four mornings per week by the end of the autumn term was never achieved. By the end of the autumn term, Nancy had decided that Janine was not ready for full student teaching, and the cooperating teacher declared that she could no longer work with Jenine – she had tried her best, and it had not worked. Nancy arranged for Jenine to repeat the pre-student teaching experience with another cooperating teacher during the winter term. The pattern of disappointment of the autumn was repeated in the winter and at the end of this term Nancy assigned a 'No Pass' grade to Jenine's field experience, terminating her status as a prospective teacher.

Was this a difficult decision for Nancy? 'Yes', she said, 'extremely difficult,' for two reasons: first, Nancy defined her teacher-educator role as helping students reach their goal of becoming a teacher. Jenine never did let go of that goal, and Nancy felt that she had failed to do her job. Second, this was a difficult decision for Nancy because the criteria for judging success or failure in a student teacher's field experience were not clear, clean and easy to judge. Especially troublesome was the question: 'When do you say "Stop, you've tried for long enough?"'

This decision was further complicated because the two women had developed an intense personal relationship around helping Jenine to make it, to learn from experience, to get it together. In this situation, it was very painful for Nancy to declare, in the end, that Jenine had failed to meet expectations and that to try again would be futile. (Nancy said that this final part of the decision process was made a bit easier as a result of Jenine becoming hostile and threatening, thus breaking the intimacy of their emotional relationship.)

Looking back, how did Nancy make sense of this drama? What did she tell herself about this situation in hindsight, and how does her understanding of the process inform us about the nature of thoughtful teaching more generally? Nancy's side of the story has four organizing themes, and perhaps they are themes that are used by other teachers when making sense of difficult and painful decisions:

1. I did what I could.
2. I was right in my perception of the situation.
3. My action prevented harm to others.
4. My action did some good.

I DID WHAT I COULD

Nancy supported her claim of having done what she could to help Jenine succeed by describing the extra efforts that she and others had made on Jenine's behalf. These tutorial support efforts began as soon as problems were noticed, and far exceeded the level of individual attention that other students in the programme received. Nancy also supported her claim of doing what she knew how to do for Jenine by giving her extra chances to make up for failure (e.g. the second pre-student teaching placement) and by changing the criteria for judging adequate progress. In the latter case, Nancy redefined the goal of Jenine's final field placement from helping this student achieve all of the special and particular ideals of a selective teacher education programme to helping her reach minimum acceptable standards in five generic domains of professional performance (i.e. instructional design, management, content knowledge, methods of teaching and professional attitude). In the end, Nancy rephrased this theme by saying, 'I did everything I knew how to do, but it didn't work.'

I WAS RIGHT IN MY PERCEPTION OF THE SITUATION

It was important to Nancy to be sure that her assessments and impressions of Jenine were accurate and fair, not the result of bias, selective perception, anxiety while under observation, or artifacts of an inappropriate field placement. Nancy did trust the testimony of her own observations and conversations with Jenine. She also determined, through conversations with the cooperating teachers, that her observations were representative of Jenine's performance more generally. Beyond confirming her own observations, Nancy saw these conversations as important to keeping both Jenine and the cooperating teachers aware of the fact that things were not going well and called for remediation. Nancy also had conversations with the director of the teacher education programme during which she sought and received support and counsel as the long decision process proceeded. Finally, Nancy cited specific examples of Jenine's unresponsiveness to feedback as evidence that this was indeed a case of a student consistently failing to meet minimum expectations for successful teaching.

In sum, Nancy pursued three avenues to validity: collecting direct evidence (well documented), reaching consensus of opinion with other observers, and validation through appeal to authority (the programme director). These latter two avenues suggest an additional professional norm: that one should consult with other professionals in difficult, non-routine cases. As Nancy said, 'I wouldn't want to make a decision like this on my own.'

MY ACTION PREVENTED HARM TO CHILDREN

Teacher-educators who evaluate the performance of student teachers are the last gatekeepers for the profession. As such, they have a moral responsibility to the generation of schoolchildren whose lives will be affected by the teacher-graduates. Nancy saw this responsibility as a fundamental, almost taken-for-granted moral imperative of her work, and she felt this responsibility when she explained that failing Jenine was the right thing to do, and the only moral thing to do, because it protected countless children from a teacher who would teach badly or not at all.

In Jenine's case, Nancy was faced with a true dilemma[1] in which a teacher-educator's responsibility to respect, teach, advise, and support a prospective teacher was at odds with the moral imperative to insure (insofar as one can) that no harm come to relatively helpless schoolchildren.

Nancy drew on her observations of Jenine in two elementary school class-rooms to resolve the dilemma. Jenine behaved selfishly in relation to the children. She was more concerned with meeting her own needs (e.g. doing college course homework in the back of the classroom) than in learning about and responding to the needs of second graders (7-year-olds). Jenine tended to blame others, including children, for problems that she herself had created or exacerbated. Jenine was physically absent from the classroom often and emotionally absent always. Providing feedback and a second chance proved insufficient to remedy these fundamental problems. Envisioning Jenine as the sole adult authority over 25 children was, in the end, terrifying to Nancy.

MY ACTION DID SOME GOOD

Finally, Nancy asserted that, for all the pain and disappointment that her decision involved, it was a very useful and good learning experience for Jenine. Nancy came to see this case, after the decision to fail Jenine was final, as the first time that Jenine had been forced to make a significant personal decision for herself and by herself – the decision about what to do with her life now that a career as a primary school teacher was foreclosed. Nancy values autonomous personal decision making and believes that a college senior should at least begin to exercise those faculties. In Nancy's reconstruction of the case it seemed good for Jenine to learn this lesson, and she felt that the lesson will probably serve Jenine well throughout her life.

It is important to highlight the fact that Nancy did not know or have reason to hope that failing Jenine would be good for her, developmentally, at the time of the decision to fail her. On the contrary, Jenine seemed ready to fall apart completely at the end of winter term. But after the 'no pass' decision was made final, Nancy continued to counsel and support Jenine, staying with her moral obligation to this devastated young woman long after she was technically obligated to do so. It was during this time that Nancy learned that Jenine had been driven to choose and stay firm in her wish to become a teacher by parental pressure. Jenine had been living out her parents' script, not her own. It was in this sense that failing Jenine provided her with the chance to begin living autonomously.

A second good result of this difficult situation was the creation of a seminar and support group within the teacher preparation programme to provide for early identification and possible remediation of problems like those that plagued Jenine. And further, Nancy has been moved to work with a colleague in supervision to create a more clear and objective set of performance criteria for judging pre-student teaching performance. What began as a clinical teaching and evaluation process for one student became a formative evaluation and development process for an entire teacher education programme.

NOTE

1   Lampert, M. (1985). How do teachers manage to teach? Perspectives on problems in practice. *Harvard Educational Review*, 55, p. 178.

Chapter 9

Case Three: No Respect for Carlos

A Hispanic student speaks of his high school experience:

> I may look like a student who doesn't like his classwork, who just
> messes off in class, but I'm not. Teachers just look at me and they
> say, 'Oh, another mess off'. I'm not dumb. They didn't care what
> was the result of my tests. I know I got a perfect score! It is like
> prejudice, but it's not prejudice . . . I just ignored it. I had this
> problem before. I had US History, but somehow my teacher didn't
> like me, I don't know why. He told me I did not belong in that
> class. And I did good on the tests. History is my best subject. I felt
> like hitting him! He said I did not have what it takes to be a
> student there. I went to my counselor and told her. Same thing.
> But you see, that made me feel mad.[1]

The moral relationship between teacher and student is more conspicuous when
it breaks down. In the quote above we can see the unraveling threads of a
relationship between adult and adolescent, between Anglo and Hispanic,
between authority and compliance, inclusion and exclusion, between learning
and alienation.

A fundamental responsibility of a teacher is to create and sustain conditions
that promote learning for *each and all* of his or her students. Teachers must
assume that every student is capable of learning. This is both a pedagogical and
a moral imperative. To meet this responsibility, teachers plan, decide, create and
reflect on conditions for learning. The basic conditions include motivation and
encouragement, knowledge of subject matter, opportunity to learn, time, space,
appropriate curricular materials, clear instruction, and methods of measuring
student learning progress. Any one of these conditions for learning, if absent or
inadequate in some way, can bring the whole learning system to a grinding halt.
Seven of these eight conditions may be in place and operating at optimal levels,
but when an eighth is missing, or weak, or selectively violated for some students,
learning is compromised and the teacher is not acting responsibly.

The Neo-Vygotskian perspective on cognitive development offers a useful
frame of reference for understanding the social, psychological and moral dynamics of school learning.[2] Three central ideas of this theory are that (1) learning is a

socially and culturally mediated process (as distinguished from a private individual process); (2) the role of teacher consists of creating conditions that enable a gradual shift of responsibility for learning from the teacher to the collective of learners; and (3) that teachers, learners and learning activities and materials must interact within the learners' 'zone of proximal development' for effective learning to take place.

Let us now use these ideas to examine the case of Carlos quoted above. What went wrong here? And what does it tell us about the personal and relational nature of teaching?

First, it seems clear that this student felt excluded from the learning group, the US History class, and that he blamed his exclusion on the teacher ('He told me I did not belong in that class.'). We do not know what the teacher intended by that statement. But whatever he intended, Carlos took it as a teacher's judgement that he did not have what it takes, intellectually speaking, to succeed or even to try to succeed in this US History class. The judgement came early, the judgement was harsh, and the judgement was at odds with Carlos' own estimate of his ability ('I'm not dumb ... History is my best subject.'). Furthermore, the teacher's delivery of this harsh judgement was gratuitous, since Carlos did stay in that section of US History for the term.

What did the teacher accomplish by his act? From a classroom management point of view, he reduced the heterogeneity and effective size of his class. While not succeeding at physically removing this 'different' student from class, he effectively removed him from complicating participation patterns by putting him in his place early on. This tactic of classroom management by selective discouragement can be inflicted in more subtle ways than we see here. To be ignored, to be ridiculed (only once), to be singled out for a 'special' pull-out programme, to be nailed with a low mark for the first assignment or test, to be segregated in the 'slow group' in the first grade (6-year-olds) – these commonplace occurrences can indeed simplify some of the work of teachers, but at great expense to the learning and lives of some students.

To create and sustain conditions that will promote learning for each and all students in a class, a responsible and effective teacher must pursue a commitment to *inclusion* as opposed to selective exclusion. He or she should ask questions like 'Who is being left out? How can I organize learning activities so that all feel included and are learning? What can I do to begin a reversal of the chain of failure experiences that some of my students have had? How can I accommodate my teaching to the full range of differences in aptitudes, learning histories, culture and dispositions that describe my students? How can we help one another to learn and change together? What do I have to learn from my students?'

These are difficult questions to answer, and they cannot be answered once and for all time. This set of questions reframes the teacher's definition of the educator's problem, and shifts the tone of teacher–student relationship from adversarial–technical to collaborative–supportive. A policy of inclusion, as reflected in sincere pursuit of answers to these questions, presupposes an attitude of respect for and genuine interest in each student and in the class as a social organism, as a learning community. As well, it requires that the teacher act both with the authority of a knowledgable adult and with the eager humility of a learner and member of a learning group.

Respect for and interest in students, in turn, are related to the moral maturity and ego development of the teacher. Adults do not ask such questions lightly, risk failure eagerly, or share power, authority, and voice without trepidation. Inclusive teaching is risky business, but the risks are worth the prize.

In Neo-Vygotskian theory the aim of good teaching is to give the game away to the learners. Through 'scaffolding' and gradual transfer of responsibility and control to the group of students, the adult teacher moves away from centre stage to become a co-participant or even an outsider in the learning community. The course may be about algebra or art or history or English. But, in this framework, schooling is also about collectively initiating, creating, and sustaining an inclusive learning community. In the long run, learning how to build learning communities may prove to be of more educative and social value than remembering disembodied academic content.

NOTES

1 Trueba, H. T. (1988) Peer socialization among minority students: A high school dropout prevention program. In H. T. Trueba and C. Delgado-Gaitan (eds), *School and society: Learning content through culture*. New York, Praeger Publishers, p. 206.

2 Cole, M. and Scribner, S. (1974) *Culture and thought: A psychological introduction*. New York: Basic Books. Wertsch, J. (1985) *Vygotsky and the social formation of the mind*. Cambridge, MA: Harvard University Press.

Reflections on Three Cases

What can we learn about the relationship between the teacher and the taught from reflecting on the stories of William, Jenine and Carlos? First, it seems clear that moral issues are intrinsic to and ubiquitous in teaching. The American principle of separation of church and state does not mean that what goes on in state schools is morally neutral. What educators and parents fear most about bad teaching and celebrate most about good teaching are manifestations of fundamental virtues. Really bad teaching is bad in a moral sense; really good teaching is good in a moral sense. No amount of technical virtuosity in instruction can compensate for or excuse morally flawed, irresponsible behaviour.

Second, morally responsible teaching is difficult, complex and sometimes painful and thankless work. Teaching is a fundamentally moral enterprise in which adults are asking and requiring children to change in directions usually dictated by adults. Understanding teaching in this light confronts the teacher with potentially unsettling questions: By what authority do I push for changes in the lives of these children? At what costs to their freedom and autonomy? Where does my responsibility for these young lives begin and end? How should I deal with true moral dilemmas in which it is simply not possible to realize two goods or avoid two evils? How much pain and discomfort am I willing to endure on behalf of my students? How are my own character weaknesses affecting the lives of others?

These questions are quite different from the questions and topics used to organize teacher education curriculum and professional development programmes for veteran teachers. Perhaps the time has come to rethink what we do in the name of teacher preparation and professional development in light of a heightened sense of the moral challenges and complexities of teaching.

Third, reflecting on these cases can give us some insight into the temptations to moral failure frequently encountered in the relationship between the teacher and the taught. Dishonesty is a common and dangerous failure for teachers and children, taking many forms and justified by motives lofty and low. Disrespect and contempt for persons or categories of persons, no matter how subtly expressed, are toxic to learning and development. Selfishness and egocentrism hurt both teachers and students. And the temptation to use morally flawed means (e.g. humiliation, segregation, violence) to achieve desired ends (e.g. order, obedience, compliance) is all too common in ordinary schools.

No single set of cases, stories and reflections can make the complexities of thoughtful teaching simple, straightforward, or unerringly good and successful. My hope is to raise questions in your minds about honesty, respect, generosity and moral scrutiny of means and ends. How do these moral virtues (or their violations) help explain life in classrooms? How can we design programmes and teach more responsibly in light of these principles? How can we serve our present society better as well as the generations to follow by taking the moral dimension of teaching as seriously as we do test scores and transcripts? For at its core, teaching is a matter of human relationships. And human relationships, whatever else they may be, are moral in character and consequence. After parent and child, the most profoundly moral relationship we and our children experience is that between the teacher and the taught.

Chapter 10

Case Four: What You Can Learn From Apple Sauce*

In mid-October I spent an autumn afternoon helping 21 first and second graders (6- and 7-year-olds) make a pot of apple sauce. The day climaxed with the great moment of tasting, when the contents of the pot, spiced with cinnamon and divided into 24 portions, were consumed with delight. Children and teacher alike declared that this was a fine and magical afternoon – one of those memorable high points that we cherish as examples of the way school should be all of the time.

At the risk of spoiling the magic by too much analysis I would like to reflect on what was learned (and could have been learned) in this classroom on an October afternoon. What can you learn from apple sauce? This question applies not only to the 6- and 7-year-olds, but also to the teacher and to me.

I've divided the list of what was learned from apple sauce into those learnings intended or anticipated by the teacher, followed by surprises and subtle side effects of the activity. Since I did not interview the teacher in advance about her plans and expectations, the line between intentions and surprises is not definitive, but rather suggestive. This would remain true even after a post hoc interview, since her direct experience of the afternoon powerfully influences recollection and reconstruction of her plans and expectations. Hopes and fears about what might happen in the future (the stuff of planning) disappear like smoke in hindsight.

ANTICIPATED LEARNINGS AND SUPPORTIVE CONDITIONS

Simply put, the two most obvious academic learning goals of apple sauce making were for the children to learn about the concept of orderly sequencing of steps in a moderately complex process and to practise expressing (through writing and drawing) an understandable description of their own activities. The former is a specific objective of the first-grade (6-years old) maths curriculum; the latter is a general aim of the language arts curriculum for both grades. They were jointly pursued through teacher-led instruction about the sequence of steps to be followed and through the children's alternately acting out the steps in the sequence and creating individual booklets describing and depicting the process.

Seven children at a time peeled and cut apples with the help and supervision of two adult volunteers, while the remaining 14 children drew pictures and wrote captions describing five steps in the apple sauce making process. After each child finished operating on one apple, he or she washed hands and returned to recipe booklet making, being replaced at one of the seven cutting boards by a classmate. During the hour or so of apple cutting and peeling, the teacher was involved in helping children (especially first-graders) spell words for their booklet captions and in directing the flow of children between their writing desks and the cutting and peeling stations. The first hour and a quarter ended with slices and chunks of 21 apples simmering in a cinnamon-spiced pot, 21 recipe booklets nearing completion, and a great wad of newspaper, peelings and apple seeds in the wastebasket. This might have been enough learning to satisfy many educators, but there was much, much more learned from this apple sauce.

Part of what else was anticipated and learned from apple sauce falls under the heading 'continuity of experience'. First, the experience of food preparation constituted a link between home and school. Young children daily see, smell and sometimes participate in food preparation in their own home kitchens. Their prior out-of-school knowledge and experiences were drawn upon in this in-school project. More proximately, the apple sauce-making activity drew on two recent school activities. The most immediate and direct connection was to a field trip to Uncle John's Cider Mill, where the children saw and smelled the process of large-scale cider making in action, and obtained apples to bring back to school. The teacher saw an opportunity for children to mentally connect their visit to orchard and cider mill with their own transformation of apples into apple sauce.

The second connection was to a prior field trip to a farmers' market, where the children purchased a variety of vegetables, brought them back to school, and made 'stone soup'. The apple sauce making project was structurally quite similar to the stone soup project (with the important difference that there was no children's literature story or folk-tale around which to organize the apple sauce making, as there was with stone soup).

In sum, this second set of intended learnings had to do with the idea (and experience) that life outside school is (or can be) connected to life in school; that school learning activities need not be segregated from one's taken for granted everyday knowledge and learning; and that transformations of a grand scale (bushels of apples into gallons of apple cider) can effectively be modelled on a manageably small scale. But this was not the whole story.

The probably anticipated but secondary student learnings from the apple sauce project had to do with safety, sanitation and satisfaction of two kinds. Learning to use a paring knife safely was intended, taught directly by modelling, tried empirically, and then backed away from when, in the judgement of the teacher, the risk of self-inflicted wounds appeared too high. (We switched to using plastic knives after the first few exciting minutes.) Nonetheless, the points were made: safety is important, sharp knives must be handled with care, and relatively mature fine-motor coordination is required to peel an apple safely with a sharp knife. The role of sanitation in food preparation was emphasized by having the children wash their hands before and after food handling. Satisfaction as an outcome of this learning activity was intended to come both from the delicious and immediate tasting of the fruits of one's own labours and from having a booklet to take home that would serve as a prop and support for a 'show and tell' conversation with parents. A subtle characteristic of these satisfactions is that they do not depend on competitiveness for success. Rather, there was 'equity of outcome', in that everyone got to contribute, everyone got to taste from the pot, and everyone got to take home a booklet. The underlying message here is that learning can be fun, delicious and communicable to an absent audience through the magic of writing. Again, for most of us, this would have been enough. But there was more to this apple sauce than is usually the case.

Apple sauce, unsurprisingly, is not all academic. The teacher intended (at least implicitly) that this set of activities would serve some social-learning functions as well. First among these was the idea that cooperation within the classroom social group could produce a delightful product that no one individual or small group could have produced. Patience in letting the project take as long as it needed to and the twin pleasures of task ownership by the children ('I'll cut my apple my way') and active, multisensory participation ('This is messy' 'That smells good!' 'Look! I cut a seed in half') were required, or at least encouraged, by the structure of the task and also hoped for as enduring, transferrable, long-term outcomes of the process. Making apple sauce may have served to make this classroom learning community happier, more cohesive, more patient, and more confident. ('If we can make apple sauce together, perhaps we can make a newspaper in the spring.')

Perhaps more could have been made of the maths and science learning potential of apple sauce. We could have weighed the apples, weighed what went into the pot, and weighed the contents of the pot after an hour of simmering, then hypothesized about how to account for the differences. We could have emphasized how halves, quarters, eighths and sixteenths are related to the whole. We could have counted seeds, dissected seeds, planted seeds, talked about nature's 'intended' role for seed and fruit. We could have demonstrated bilateral and cross-sectional symmetry. (Have you ever cut an apple in half the 'wrong way?' Try it: there is a delightful surprise within.) We could have taught juggling, or given examples of the roles of the apple in religion, myth, literature, and the economy of Michigan. We did none of these things, although I would not be surprised if the apple example arises again when large fractions are studied in maths.

SURPRISES AND SIDE EFFECTS

What did the teacher learn more generally about herself and about teaching from apple sauce? From her response to seeing the apparent danger of sharp knives in little hands, she learned something about her own tolerance for risk in the name of learning. In this case, the risk of injury appeared substantial, the particular learning aim of successful use of paring knives was marginal, and a safer alternative (plastic knives) was at hand. But it is interesting that the need for revision of this important detail of the apple sauce-making plan did not arise during pre-active planning, but only in the vividness of action. Perhaps this was a case of overgeneralization from the accident-free stone soup project, in which various vegetables were sliced and diced using the same sharp set of paring knives. What became clear as the first seven children began working on their apples was that it is considerably easier to slice a celery stalk or a carrot than it is to peel an apple.

The teacher and I also learned something about the necessity of detailed planning of a complex activity. In this case, the planning challenge was to design a pair of activities that were substantively connected, academically defensible, and robust enough to be sustained in the face of internal interruptions (i.e. the children's continual shifting from drawing and writing to apple peeling and then back again to drawing and writing). It was also crucial to carrying out this plan that the teacher have one or two adult helpers, and the manifest success of the activity confirmed (for the teacher) the wisdom of seeking help in this kind of teaching. A final lesson learned (or reconfirmed) by the teacher was that, especially with young children, resolution of a cause-and-effect process during a single afternoon is quite satisfying. Beginning the afternoon with a bag of apples and ending the day with one's own recipe booklet and the taste of warm apple sauce fits the attention span of 6- and 7-year-olds quite nicely. Multiday projects may make sense later in the year.

Two subtle but important lessons about individual student differences and about gender roles were learned from apple sauce. Some children who had various difficulties with reading or with verbal participation in group activities positively shone at apple cutting and peeling. They acted confidently and competently, even helping classmates learn how to cut and peel. The activity structure made it possible for them to thrive in the same classroom and group in which they typically struggle. Teacher, adult volunteers, and children noticed these individual differences to different degrees, and the consequences of this consciousness raising will take time to manifest themselves. But for now, it is worth noting that these insights would not have arisen in the context of more verbally loaded classroom activities. The issue of gender roles was subtle in that the question of whether it was appropriate for boys to be so involved in food preparation never came up. Boys and girls together pitched in and got the job done. One can only hope that this egalitarian approach will continue throughout the children's school experiences.

CONCLUSION

In conclusion, more was learned from apple sauce than at first meets the eye. The planning, acting, revising and happy resolution of the apple sauce-making activity affected everyone involved. Academic, social, and professional development learning potentials were realized in subtle and obvious ways. Reflection on the experience suggested additional curriculum potential that may be realized next year by this teacher and her students, or at any time by other teachers and students. And learnings about teaching, activity structures, and individual students may continue to influence this teacher's planning for the remainder of the school year. General abstract principles – such as continuity of experience, equity of outcomes, multi-ability task demands, comprehensive planning, flexible revision of plans, and sensitivity to developmental capabilities of schoolchildren – take on vividness and new meaning when depicted in the garb of a concrete, visualizable classroom activity. And I, for one, will never be able to see an apple in the same simple light as I did in the days before learning from apple sauce.

* Reprinted by permission of the publisher from E. Eisner and A. Peshkin (eds) *Qualitative Inquiry in Education*. New York: Teachers College Press, (c) 1990 by Teachers College, Columbia University. All rights reserved, pp. 327–32.

Chapter 11

Case Five: Mixed Messages About Diary Time

with Susan Florio-Ruane

Student diaries – perhaps you have thought about them or tried them in your classroom, or even been required to keep a journal as a student. There are many reasons to encourage diary keeping. Diaries provide opportunities to reflect on past experience and to focus that reflection by writing. Diary writing can be private, avoiding concern about an audience's scrutiny. Yet when student dairies are shared, they afford teachers a glimpse of the thoughts and feelings of their students. So why not plan a classroom diary time?

If this sounds too simple to you, you are not alone. When diaries are written within institutional settings such as the classroom, their potential as a perfect window on the mind is compromised by the realities of school life. Most obviously, diaries written in school are not written in privacy. They are often initiated, not by the diarist but by the teacher. And since most writing done at school has an audience, the issue of audience in classroom diaries is, at best, uncertain.

This case examines the social complexities of diary writing in one primary school classroom (a combined second and third grade; 7- and 8-year-olds), in the form of a life history of diary time across the school year. This is not a recipe for how to keep classroom diaries. Instead, it portrays the opportunities and limits of diary writing in an ordinary classroom, and the thoughtfulness required of a teacher who initiates this seemingly straightforward activity.

THE LIFE HISTORY OF DIARY TIME

Our first interview with Ms Donovan, the second/third grade teacher in Room 12, took place on 5 September, the day before the school year began. She told us that this year she planned to have her students write in diaries for the last 10 or 15 minutes of each school day, and that she planned to use that time herself to write in the journal that she was keeping as part of our research project. She intended to write in a 'stream of consciousness' fashion. Field notes written on the same day record that as Ms Donovan drafted a model daily schedule, she allotted the final 10 minutes of the day to diary time. Ms Donovan commented that having her students write in diaries was something she had wanted to do for years and that her participation in the research project would 'give added impetus' to her to do it.

Getting Started

On the first day of school, diary time was expanded to fill the final hour of the day. This was to allow time for Ms Donovan to introduce her plan, to teach about the form and purposes of diary keeping, and for the children to make and decorate cardboard covers for their diaries and to write their first entries. Following afternoon recess, at about 2:15 pm, Ms Donovan had the children sit on the carpet in a filled circle. The field notes pick up the story:

> Looking up at the chalkboard where the schedule had been written, one child said, 'It's almost time for diary'. Another child said, 'What's that?' Ms Donovan said, 'That's what we have to discuss. Some kids don't know what it is yet.'
>
> Proceeding, Ms Donovan asked, 'Does anyone know what a diary is?'

> *Linda:*   Things that you write down that you think of
>
> *Kathy:*   Private
>
> *Sarah:*   That you think are important

After taking some comments from the floor, Ms Donovan noted that 'no two diaries are the same'. Anthony chimed in at this point: 'I already have a diary with a key and lock.' There was a discussion about why one might lock a diary. The issue of privacy was highlighted, and Ms Donovan said, 'I don't want to read them unless you want to share them with me or with the class.' She offered to lock them in a filing cabinet drawer.

Dani asked, 'How do you correct them?'

Ms Donovan said that they were not to be corrected and that she, too, would have one.

Considerable time was spent constructing the diaries, and the procedure had the following parts:

1. The diary covers were to be decorated with crayon or magic marker.
2. Children who finished decorating ahead of time were not to begin writing in the diaries but were to take a worksheet and complete it. The worksheets were mazes and the children were told they could colour them. They were told the mazes would be 'corrected'.

3. Children were to decorate their diaries with picture(s) of favourite things. Then the diaries were filled with five sheets of lined paper.

4. The third grade paper was distinguished from the second grade paper (they are essentially the same except that third grade paper has narrower spaces between the lines).

5. When the children asked what would happen when they finished using the five pages, they were told that they could 'make a new one'.

Ms Donovan gave an example of the cover illustration for the diary. She drew a Christmas tree. Three children drew Christmas trees too. Other covers included: bicycles, a star that evolved into the emblem of the Dallas Cowboys, a house, a cat, a swing set and a tree.

Once the covers were underway, Ms Donovan passed out the 'third grade paper' and asked the researcher to pass out the 'second grade paper'. Then the children began to write in their diaries as Ms Donovan circulated, stapling the booklets together. There were several procedural directives as the writing began:

1. With regard to privacy, Ms Donovan said that you shouldn't ask other people what they are writing.

2. Regarding help with spelling words, Ms Donovan said that she would also be writing in her diary and not looking up and around the room. Therefore, students should come up to her table if they needed help. Ms Donovan said that the researcher would be available to help as well. The researcher decided to write in her field note journal during diary writing time. Much like during Uninterrupted Silent Reading (USR), Ms Donovan and the fieldworker both modelled the process and perhaps enabled it by this strategy.

3. Ms Donovan said that she would share part of what she was writing in her diary (i.e. that she has a good class and has had a good day). The rest, she said, 'is for me'. She also pointed out that diary time 'was sort of like USR but was UW (Uninterrupted Writing), so that you can think and write down your thoughts by yourself'. She added that 'if you can't think of anything, write the word "write" until you can think of an idea.'

During diary time, some children came to the fieldworker with scraps of paper and asked her to spell words for them. The first was Stan. He had a full sheet of third grade paper and said that he would keep the words she spelled for him in a list so that he could remember them. He said that he did this last year with his second grade teacher. Some of the children came with questions about what to write (e.g. Do you write about 'just school', or can you write about 'before school?').

During the diary writing time there was not much talk among the students. For the first time some children put up tall books or workbooks around their papers as visual barriers. There appeared to be much concern for privacy and the students did not hasten to show their entries to Ms Donovan. Writing went on this way from 2:50 until 3:00.

At 3:01, Ms Donovan asked the children to stop. She asked, 'How many people had a hard time thinking of things to write about?' She suggested that anybody who didn't should give them some ideas. (She was apparently aware of Chet, the boy who had the most trouble thinking of something to write. He had come to the fieldworker for help in decorating his cover. When she suggested that he might want to write something inside, he said he did not know what to write. Attempting to get him started, she discovered that he is new in town, has yet to make many friends, and therefore felt he did not have much to recount. Ms Donovan addressed much of the post-writing discussion to Chet, looking at him a lot.) Ms Donovan asked the class, 'How do you think of things to write?' She called on two boys who seemed to have no trouble making entries.

Joseph: I thought.

Anthony: I don't know.

Ms Donovan said, 'It isn't easy to talk about. I had a hard time also.' But she suggested topics such as 'what you liked about today', 'what you didn't like about today', and 'how you felt'.

How do you feel right now, at the end of the day?' The students said that they were 'tired', that they 'wanted to stay some more'. Saying that they could write about these feelings and that she didn't want to 'cut them off', Ms Donovan promised that there would be more time tomorrow. She let those that wanted to continue writing to do so for a few minutes but began to collect the diaries and put them in her filing cabinet.

Diary writing was followed by a very brief clean up and dismissal.

Discussion

Diary time was clearly a planned occasion for writing that originated with the teacher. By alloting a regular daily time slot for diary writing even before she met her students and by discussing her intentions with the researchers, Ms Donovan made a commitment to establish this activity as a routine. On 5 September we had no detailed plan or picture of what diary time would be like, or of what purposes the teacher thought it would serve for her students. But Ms Donovan's scheduling of diary time as the very last activity of the day and her expressed desire to write in her own journal at that time suggest a picture of a quiet period of private reflection and writing about the major events of the day, during which each child would be in his or her own little world for a while. But the realities of the classroom transformed this picture in many unforseen ways. The story of the first diary time makes visible some of the usually hidden facets of thoughtful teaching. We address them under the headings of planning, implementation, audience and function.

Planning. Diary time was clearly a teacher-originated and teacher-planned activity, as distinguished from student-initiated activities, mandated curricular activities, or unexpected serendipitous events. Ms Donovan told us in advance of her intention to have the students write daily diary entries. She allocated a full hour of the important first day of school to diary time and budgeted 10 minutes at the end of each daily schedule for diary writing. Her comments on the day before school began and her actions during the first diary time indicate that she had wanted to have her students keep diaries for some years, that she had never done so before, and that she thought it would be a valuable activity for the children. Her participation in a study of written literacy, including keeping a journal herself, provided added impetus to institute diary time, serving her needs as well as the children's. In short, it was important to Ms Donovan that diary time succeed.

Much of Ms Donovan's planning for diary time must be inferred. Like other experienced elementary teachers whose planning has been studied, she did not write out an elaborate, step-by-step plan book entry for diary time. The only written record of planning for the first diary time is the two-word entry on the schedule for that day. Yet her comments recorded in 5 September interview and field notes, her elaborate communication of the diary time plan to her students, and the fact that materials for making diary covers were ready when needed all indicate that Ms Donovan had a detailed plan worked out in her imagination – she was not simply improvising. Although she had put a good deal of thought into her preparations for diary time, this thinking was invisible to outside observers.

Implementation. Life in classrooms is unpredictable. Activities rarely are implemented exactly as planned. The discrepancy between plan and action is especially likely to be visible in the early days and weeks of school, when teacher and students are first getting to know one another, and also when a teacher is trying out an activity for the first time. The first diary time met both of these conditions, and Ms Donovan adjusted her plan to accommodate the unpredictable. In the orientating discussion of what diaries are, she built on student contributions of ideas about the purposes and contents of diary entries. The discussion of privacy was triggered by a student commenting that he owned a diary with a lock and key. Ms Donovan asked for help in handing out paper from the fieldworker and offered her services in helping with spelling – something that neither of them had planned. Implementation of Ms Donovan's plan depended heavily on her interactive decision-making and flexibility in building on student contributions. The plan was tailored to fit the moment rather than the moment forced to fit the structure of the plan.

Another feature of plan implementation worth mentioning is Ms Donovan's use of modelling. She modelled both the decoration of a diary cover and the diary writing process itself. Further, she shared one part of her own diary entry with the class, but told them that the remainder of the entry was private ('just for me'), showing that each writer was to be the judge of what to share and what to keep secret. Her use of modelling showed up in various ways in other occasions for writing throughout the year. The first diary time is the earliest example of a pattern of modelling in which the emphasis is on making explicit how the teacher is thinking about and doing the writing task herself, rather than telling the student what the 'right way' to do the task is. Implicit in this approach are the teacher's concern that students learn and attend to the processes of thought and action as well as to the products of writing, sufficient respect for the meaningful-ness of the task that the teacher herself will enter into it as a full participant, and an openness to accept decisions by individual students to approach the task in a way that is different from that modelled by the teacher (as long as they do participate).

Diary time, as implemented, guaranteed success for every student. The activity combined design and construction, art work, oral discussion and writing. Every student was able to make and decorate a personalized diary cover, and to participate as a listener or speaker in the discussion of what diaries are and how they can be useful. Even those who did not write anything had a concrete, visible product to show for the first day of school. Furthermore, the cover decorations were to be pictures of 'favourite things' – a way for students to think about, declare and make public some personal information. Some success for all students was built in to the activity, and the link between drawing and writing was manifested on the first day of school.

Finally, it is clear that implementation of the first diary time was also the beginning of Ms Donovan's planning for the second and subsequent diary times. She paid attention to the unanticipated problems that cropped up and imme-diately began thinking of ways to solve these problems. After the children were dismissed Ms Donovan wrote a journal entry of her own that was both a reflection on diary time and a plan for improving the process the following day. In her reflection and planning, Ms Donovan identified two problems: children inter-rupting to ask how to spell words and some children not being able to think of what to write about. She came up with an idea for how to solve the second of these:

> Discussed writing a diary; emphasized idea of personal thoughts and importance of privacy. Most caught on quickly ... some kept their own diaries at home.
>
> I had planned to keep my journal while the class works in theirs, but for the first few weeks it will be difficult to accomplish with their interruptions for spelling and ideas.
>
> Tomorrow I'll read short selections from logs and journals kept by such people as Anne Frank and Washington Irving and have the children figure out how they have become useful for us and possibly give them some ideas. I'll have some share their entries from yesterday if they wish, then pull a small group to work out some strategies to help them think of what to write.

Especially in a continuing activity like diary time, the teacher played the roles of observant and reflective critic of her own teaching, problem solver and formative evaluator of classroom processes, and leader, instructor and facilitator of learning activities. Today's reflections become tomorrow's plans.

Audience. Who was the audience for the student diaries? At one level the teacher intended that the young diarists themselves would be their own audience. The discussion of privacy and the seriousness with which the teacher and students protected their own diaries lend support to the idea of 'author as audience'. But, at the same time, there is reason to think that both teacher and children saw Ms Donovan and the whole class as potential audience for diary entries. 'Teacher as audience' was supported by the facts that diary keeping was a teacher-imposed task, that she knew and taught 'the rules' for diary keeping, that she read aloud a part of her first journal entry, and that the teacher collected and stored the diaries in her locked filing cabinet. Student concerns about correct spelling, questions about how the teacher will 'correct them' and teacher assistance for those who could not think of what to write also suggest that the teacher was an important audience. Peers were introduced as potential audience by Ms Donovan's comment that 'I don't want to read them unless you want to share them with me or the class'.

The children appeared to be a bit confused by the mixed message of privacy, on the one hand, and teacher and peers as audience on the other. The diary writing activity could be seen as an invitation to engage in two incompatible tasks: 1) private, freewheeling writing intended for the author's eyes only, in which description and reflection were of paramount importance, and errors of form, spelling, or grammar were of no consequence, and 2) 'correct' writing about one's daily experiences and feelings, that fits the conventions of diary entries as a literary form and the standards of neatness, spelling, punctuation, coherence and length of school writing tasks that please the teacher. Taking the perspective of a 7- or 8-year-old child on the first day of school, there seem to be three ways to resolve this dilemma:

1. Treat diary time as just another school writing task, and write what you think will please the teacher. Get help from an adult with spelling words and with further clarification of 'the rules'.
2. Treat diary time as a private, reflective writing task in which the usual rules of school writing are mercifully suspended.
3. Write nothing. Let the teacher remove all of the ambiguity from this new kind of writing task by helping you to think of what and how to write.

Some children responded in each of these ways to diary time. Ambiguity about audience in a student writing activity affected both the students' interpretations of the task and the content of their writing in diverse ways.

Function. Initially, the planned function of diary time was to have children reflect on the events of the day and to become aware of their feelings and thoughts about school life, as evidenced by Ms Donovan's scheduling diary time as the last activity of the day and her expressed desire to write reflectively in her journal while the students wrote in theirs. Ms Donovan held the same reflective goals for herself as for her students, as she wrote in an early journal entry:

> Sharing this journal and my thoughts during the week with another (the researcher) on a scheduled basis is helping me to reflect in a less nebulous manner on planning and assessment of lessons. By articulating my conceptions and beliefs, it has become easier for me to present ideas in a more logical manner with fewer inconsistencies. I wonder if the children will develop greater oral ease through writing and reflecting on their ideas? (*Journal*, 9 November 1979)

The first diary time gave each child a chance to succeed at constructing and decorating a diary – a visible product of the first day of school. Furthermore, the decorations on the diary covers expressed information about each child's 'favourite things' that was useful to the teacher and to the children, as they jointly went about building the classroom social system – getting the year off to a good start by getting to know one another.

The investment of a full hour of the first day of school in diary time communicated to the children that writing was to be an important part of life in this classroom, and that Ms Donovan would do whatever is necessary to insure that everyone would write. Providing the correct spelling of words and her plan to work with small groups who could not think of anything to write are examples of her determination to have every student participate, even at the expense of journal writing time for herself.

Beyond communicating teacher expectations about writing in Room 12, the first diary time also served as a diagnostic writing assessment. Ms Donovan learned, sometimes to her surprise, which students had difficulty writing. She learned that all of her students were concerned with correct spelling, even though the teacher-intended audience was the individual writer. She also learned that the concept of a diary and the personal and historical functions it can serve were not well understood by the children, and she formed a plan to fill this gap of knowledge and motivation. As well, Ms Donovan began to learn about the amount and kind of teacher energy it would take to introduce, implement, and maintain a complex, long-term occasion with this particular class.

Finally, diary time served a managerial function: to calm down students at the end of the school day and to end the day on a reflective, academically justifiable note. The comparison of diary writing to Uninterrupted Silent Reading (USR) that Ms Donovan made when introducing the first diary time is telling. Ms Donovan had used USR following recess and lunch to calm the children and to focus them on an individual academic task as they returned to the classroom, one-by-one or two-by-two. Diary time (or Uninterrupted Writing) served as closure and transition between school and home, just as USR was intended to ease the transition between active, social, out-of-classroom activity and calmer, individual in-class academic activity.

The Complexity of Diary Writing in School

Diary time was an occasion for writing that did not live up to all of Ms Donovan's hopes and expectations. Even so, it offered several benefits to the students, the teacher and the researchers. In the year that we observed Ms Donovan's class, diary time was launched for the first time, which often amounts to a pilot test. While only partially successful in living up to Ms Donovan's hopes, diary time yielded several insights into her thinking about writing, instruction and the classroom learning setting. In a sense, the life history of diary time is an opportunity to experience that pilot test vicariously and to think about its implications for one's own teaching.

For all the instructional soundness of diary time, the seeds of its ultimate difficulties were present at the outset. Despite teacher planning and support, diary time, like many classroom activities, took on a life of its own as the year progressed. By year's end, about six children were still keeping diaries in school, but they were doing so as independent activity during free time. The field notes show by early October the regular 10-minute slot for diary time was shifted to various parts of the day. By January it had disappeared from the daily schedule.

What were the difficulties in sustaining diary time? Ms Donovan had some ideas on this in an interview one year later:

> Originally I had hoped to write a diary at the same time the
> children did, but it didn't work out too well. Because even though
> there was the idea of the diaries being private and no one had to
> read them except them and that they were just for their own use,
> they still wanted to spell the words correctly and have it so it had

some form to it. And they would have to come up and ask me to
spell a lot of the words. I couldn't write in my diary very much.
And then ... we tried to set a special time aside every day and
that just got to be almost impossible because of the way the
schedule of the day goes .... So, from wanting to write every day
it went to three times a week and then it sort of just died out after
a while because it was one of those activities that was real
difficult to fit in.

   Another problem with it was that the children had a real
difficult time reflecting back on what they had done .... Even if
you gave them a topic to write about, they wanted to write about
what happened in their lives but they didn't think their lives were
very interesting .... Most of the kids at the end of the year
weren't writing in diaries. (Interview, 9 August 1980)

In making sense of the decline and fall of diary time, Ms Donovan cites factors
related both to the private mental lives of the children and to the situational
context. Her inferences that the children had difficulty reflecting and did not
think their lives were very interesting derive from her observations of student
behaviour. Diary time was plagued by the children's concerns about correct
spelling and by the common lament that they did not know what to write. This
state of affairs seems paradoxical when the diary is seen as a private personal
written form. Yet when diary writing is brought into the classroom context, it
becomes apparent that the children's concerns make sense, given the expectations about school writing in general, and the status of diary time as part of the
day's scheduled activities. Living with this paradox, student writers became
stalled, and so did Ms Donovan. It comes as no surprise, then, that diary time lost
its priority in a daily schedule filled with a myriad of other more conventional
instructional activities.

   From the outset, diary time contained a number of conflicting messages
regarding privacy, correctness and audience. Different students approached the
task in different ways that ultimately related to whether the diary functioned for
them as private written reflection or as public sharing of thoughts in written
form. Some of Ms Donovan's efforts to communicate her plan for diary time and
support its continuation contributed to the ambiguity.

Modelling

Ms Donovan provided models for the children of several forms. First, she made a
model diary with decorated cover for the children. Second, she hoped to write in
her own journal during diary time, thus modelling the process. And third, she
brought sample diary entries from published diaries to class to share when the
children seemed to have difficulty getting started. Modelling provided both a
prop and a standard, and in so doing both enabled and limited the students' diary

writing. A number of children copied Ms Donovan's diary cover design, getting the task done, but revealing nothing about their 'favourite things'. The sharing of the published diary entries, while illustrative in their content and form, conveyed that diaries are not necessarily private and that there might be standards for what constitutes an appropriate diary entry (despite the teacher's assertion that no one need share them). Finally, because of contextual constraints, Ms Donovan did not have the uninterrupted privacy she needed to write in her own journal during diary time. Thus an important part of the modelling process was unavailable.

Audience and Concern for Correctness

Diary time was to be writing that was private and personal. It was intended to stimulate writing and reflection unconstrained by worries about correctness, audience and evaluation. It was to be a chance to practice thinking on paper. Yet a second look at diary time shows that it had most of the trappings of writing as academic performance: diary time was initiated by the teacher and given regularly scheduled status. Diaries were collected and kept in the teacher's locked file cabinet. While this was intended to ensure privacy, it is worth noting that only tests, notebooks and other official written materials were kept here, and that the children did not have access to their diaries unless Ms Donovan unlocked the cabinet. Diaries were written on official school paper that differed by year. Although not required, spelling correctness was reinforced by the adults' willingness to interrupt their own writing to help the children spell.

The first five diary entries of Jane, a third grader, shows that many features of diary time resembled formal academic writing rather than private written reflection. Jane was a prolific writer who eventually offered to share her diary with the fieldworker. At first, Jane wrote at some length about things that had happened to her outside school and classroom. She experimented with audience by initially personifying the diary and addressing it directly ('Dear Diary'). Her second entry had no such direct address, but her third again resembles the 'letter to my diary' format in that it includes a closing ('I better go! Bye!'). By the fourth day of school, however, Jane begins her diary entry in the form the students are requested to begin all of their written work in Ms Donovan's class: with her name just opposite the date.

Another change in Jane's diary entries occurs on the fourth day. Many children had been having difficulty deciding what to write. Ms Donovan's suggestions limited the scope of the writing to what was going on in school (e.g. what you liked about today; what you didn't like about today; how you felt). While this strategy was intended to help children not writing as fluently as Jane, she had begun to learn by Day 4 that school topics were the most appropriate for diary entries. Her entries changed in their subjects and length after the first three days to become decidedly more school-related and terse.

In a paradoxical way, the more support Ms Donovan provided in the form of models, protected time for diary writing, ensured safekeeping of the diaries, and help with spelling, the further from the original intent of diary writing the class moved. Faced with ambiguity about purpose, audience and format, the students increased their pursuit of help from the teacher, the teacher continued to support the task, and a cycle began that moved most of the children far from diary writing by the end of the first month of school.

Diary time reveals complexity of two sorts. It shows the complexity of the writing process, where privacy and audience stand in a figure/ground relationship that shifts, depending on the author's intentions and the conventions of the genre. In addition, diary time illustrates the complexity of an ordinary classroom as a setting for writing. In diary time, there are social norms embedded in classroom life that limit the forms and functions of writing. Those norms give meaning both to the material environment (lined paper, filing cabinet, daily schedule) and to the social relations that constitute everyday school life (e.g. teacher as authority and evaluator). It was difficult for the teacher and the children to re-cast their usual ways of behaving and making sense of writing in school in the service of diary time.

All of these complexities contributed to the mixed success and eventual demise of diary time. Yet we can learn something by reflecting on those difficulties. Most obviously, social context is profoundly involved in the writing process as students seek to discover the purposes, audience, and consequences of their writing. Many subtle facets of the classroom environment contribute to the sense that the children will make of a writing task and to the richness of the writing itself. Implements, materials, time and space all play powerful parts in school writing activities. In addition, the teacher may be variously defined as the initiator, helper, critic or audience of school writing. The way his or her role is defined has implications for the students' social identity as well. Re-definition of the roles of teacher and students, no matter how subtle or bold, require attention and negotiation. In the end, because of such complexity, not every innovation will look precisely like what the teacher had in mind, and not every one will capture the imagination and energy of every student. But even partially successful attempts at improving classroom tasks will bear fruit when, examined in retrospect, they inform the continuing process of setting realistic goals, planning meaningful activities and learning from experience.

PART FOUR

CULTIVATING THOUGHTFUL TEACHING

The metaphor of cultivating thoughtful teaching brings images of farming and gardening to mind. When we cultivate, we act intentionally to shape, control and pay careful attention to that which is growing. Anthropologists mark the beginnings of civilization at the time when early humans began to cultivate crops, shifting gradually away from nomadic hunting and gathering. Cultivation requires planning, cooperation, working for delayed gratification, and commitment to care of a particular tract of land. Cultivating thoughtful teaching calls for similar investments of attention, foresight, effort and patient commitment. We don't become more thoughtful by merely 'having experiences'. Rather, we can begin to become more thoughtful teachers by questioning and reflecting, actively making sense of our experiences, and working to see the connections between our close-at-hand environment and larger ideas and frameworks.

This final section includes chapters that deal with three questions: how can teacher-educators become more thoughtfully critical of the ways we prepare beginners? How might individual teachers take control of and responsibility for their own professional development? And, how might veteran teachers profit from working with novices?

BETTER QUESTIONS

This chapter is my attempt to practise what I preach about the proper role of research as *service* to teachers. How can researchers who study and describe the mental landscape of teaching – their planning, implicit theories, decisions and dilemmas – give genuine service to the teachers of teachers? What does all this theory offer that is practical? My answer, in two words, is 'better questions': questions about learning to teach and nurturing beginners that would never have arisen before the advent of research on teacher thinking. These are still good questions for thoughtful teacher-educators to ask of our contemporary teacher preparation programmes and practices. And they are also good questions for teachers of children to ask about yourselves, your students, and your hopes and plans.

TEACHERS AS DESIGNERS

Cultivating thoughtful teaching must begin at the beginning, in sound teacher preparation. But it must not stop there. Knowledge of subject matter, habits of mind, technical skills of instruction and curriculum design, and applied theories of learning and development have plenty of room for growth on a new teacher's graduation day, and, indeed, on the day of his or her 10th or 20th anniversary in the profession. Cultivating thoughtful teaching is a career-long process of personal and professional development, and of accommodating general principles and concepts to the continually varying particulars of your school, your students, your own changing personality and life circumstances.

'Teachers As Designers in Self-Directed Professional Development' is a call for practising teachers to take initiative and responsibility for the content and direction of their own career-long learning and growth. Cultivating your own mind and manner of good teaching is a professional responsibility that you dare not delegate. Instead, I propose seven principles of design to guide your vital and personal work of self-directed professional development.

THOUGHTFUL MENTORING

If you really want to understand something, try teaching it to someone else. This holds true for playing a violin, writing a poem, factoring an equation, or explaining photosynthesis. It is also true of teaching itself. Supervising a novice learning to teach takes a veteran teacher back to the basics, and back in time to his or her own initiation. Unpacking the taken for granted complexities of school life and explaining your reasons for teaching as you do can have two important audiences: the eager student teacher and also the experienced veteran. Mentoring at its best is a two-way relationship.

This chapter lays out some of the ways that veteran teachers learn from beginners. Crucial to most learning, of course, is to expect that you do indeed have something to learn from a person or experience, and to act on that expectation. Seeking opportunities to act simultaneously as a teacher of children and a teacher-educator, and listening critically as you explain yourself and your world, can go a long way towards sustaining thoughtfulness in your teaching.

As with the earlier sections of this book, I think of these chapters as points of departure for thoughts, conversations, and local initiatives to make school a better place for children and adults.

Chapter 12

Asking Better Questions About Teacher Preparation

The field of research on teacher thinking is thriving and growing. But what is not so clear is how (or whether) this research can be informative and useful to teacher educators. What conditions must be satisfied in order to move from the literature on teacher thinking to more thoughtful teaching and teacher education? And what steps have already been taken to realize some of the practical promise of teacher thinking research? This chapter explores these questions within the larger framework of the relationship between research and practice in education.

There are three ways to characterize the relationship between research on teaching, on the one hand, and teacher education, on the other hand. In the worst case, research on teaching has *no* relationship at all to the practice of teacher education. Researchers pursue their own narrow and parochial interests, publish in obscure language in obscure journals, and avoid all discussion of practical implications of their work. For their part, teacher-educators see this kind of research as irrelevant and impossible to understand, and continue to use unexamined habits and traditional ways of preparing teachers.

A second and better kind of relationship between research on teaching and teacher education follows from research in the Process–Product tradition. Teacher effectiveness researchers see the role of research as to discover those behaviours, skills, patterns and strategies that lead to improved student learning and achievement. In this framework, the implications for teacher education are rather direct: train prospective teachers to behave in the ways that research has shown to be most effective in producing achievement gains in students. The principal role of the teacher-educator in this relationship is that of trainer of students in the skills and strategies empirically endorsed by the research community. This is an essentially top-down model in which researchers and the knowledge they produce govern the content and practice of teacher preparation.

In this second kind of relationship between research and practice there are teacher-educators who have read one or two reviews of the literature of teacher thinking, who have attended conference presentations of this research, or who have colleagues who are engaged in studies of teacher thinking. These teacher-educators may have a felt sense that there is some potential in this work for affecting their conduct of teacher preparation, but may not know quite what to do about it. Some are awaiting a hypothetical 'Phase 2' of research on teacher thinking, when researchers move from description of the ways teachers think to quasi-experiments and other tough-minded designs from which prescriptions will flow for how teachers ought to think, plan and decide. These teacher-educators wait in vain. Research on teacher thinking will never provide a scientific basis for prescribing how teachers ought to think.

A third kind of relationship between research on teaching (particularly research on teacher thinking) and the practice of teacher education exists only in potential. In this relationship members of the research community behave as *consultants* to the community of teacher-educators. To work well as a consultant one must come to see the client's (teacher-educator's) problems from the per-spective of a sympathetic insider. A good consultant has expertise and a perspective different from that of the client, and engages this expertise in the service of the client's own ends. A consultant seldom solves major problems, but often contributes important pieces to the client's own solutions. The best con-sultants are those who leave something interesting and provocative to think about as the clients continue to wrestle with the complexities of the local problematic situation. What this third relationship entails is a more humble and service-oriented role for research on teaching in relation to teacher education; a relationship in which researchers provide food for thought responsive to the perceived needs of teacher-educators. This kind of a relationship holds great promise for research on teacher thinking as a source of valuable assistance in the thoughtful preparation of teachers.

In this third kind of relationship we have teacher-educators who have learned a bit about research on teacher thinking, who have experienced the felt sense that something ought to be done with this work, and who have begun to think about their teaching of novices in light of new descriptions of the way teaching is. These teacher- educators are not waiting for researchers to tell them what to do next. Some have begun applied research programmes of their own. Others have begun to make small changes in the content of their teaching and in the ways that they teach. Still others have begun the demanding and politically complicated process of reorganizing whole teacher preparation programmes to reflect their collective and emergent sense of what constitutes progress in teacher education. These are the leaders and risk takers in teacher education to whom research on teacher thinking can be most useful.

FOUR GENERAL CLAIMS

Given this way of thinking about the relationship of research and practice, consider the following four general claims about the promise of research on teacher thinking for influencing teacher education:

1. Research on teacher thinking has small but important contributions to make to the practice of teacher education. Research on teacher thinking does not constitute the ground for *radical* revision of the form and content of teacher preparation. Some of the most important contributions to teacher education may take the form of rationalizing, justifying and understanding practices that have long been in place in teacher education. Furthermore, many contributions of research on teacher thinking will not make teacher education easier, but they may make teacher preparation more interesting.

2. The study of the thoughts, knowledge and dispositions of *experienced* teachers (important as this is) does not answer the questions of what novices should be taught and how they should be prepared. There are two interrelated problems here: a) most of this research describes teacher thinking, planning, and decision-making without taking an empirically supported position on the effectiveness or desirability of these forms and patterns of teacher thinking; and, b) even if these forms of teacher thinking are shown to be desirable for teachers, it remains to be discovered how one might best help start inexperienced prospective teachers moving in these directions.

3. Particular changes and improvements made in the content and process of teacher preparation ought to be invented, tested and adapted by teacher-educators themselves. Research on teacher thinking can provide examples of concepts, methods and food for thought for teacher-educators, but *not* well-defined prescriptions for how to educate teachers. (The ideal situation is when researchers on teacher thinking themselves become practising teacher educators and learn how to apply their research to their own teaching.)

4. Fourth, research on teacher thinking has already begun to affect the ways that teacher-educators think and act while preparing novices for the teaching profession. Teacher-educators are asking thoughtful questions about the content and process of their work and, in the last five years, a number of interesting and encouraging programme innovations have been started with still more in the planning stages. To date, research on teacher thinking has perhaps affected the ways in which teachers are prepared more visibly than it has affected the ways teachers teach in classrooms.

THINKING FROM THE RESEARCH

Suppose that a researcher on teacher thinking is invited to consult with a faculty of teacher-educators. What could he or she offer as food for thought to these teacher-educators as they think about strengthening their own teacher preparation programme? Ideas extrapolated from research on teacher thinking that such a consultant could offer in response to the teacher-educators' needs are offered below under three headings: Preconceptions and Implicit Theories, Planning and Reflection, and Dilemmas and Uncertainty.

PRECONCEPTIONS AND IMPLICIT THEORIES

Research on teacher thinking has documented the fact that teachers develop and hold implicit theories about their students (Bussis, Chittenden and Amarel, 1976), about the subject matter that they teach (Ball, 1986; Duffy, 1977; Elbaz, 1981; Kuhs, 1980) and about their roles and responsibilities and how they should act (Ignatovich, Cusick and Ray, 1979; Olson, 1981). These implicit theories are not neat and complete reproductions of the educational psychology found in textbooks or lecture notes. Rather, teachers' implicit theories tend to be eclectic aggregations of cause-effect propositions from many sources, rules of thumb, generalizations drawn from personal experience, beliefs, values, biases and prejudices. Teachers are subject to the full range of insights and errors in human judgement described by Nisbett and Ross (1980), just as all humans are when faced with complex, fast-paced, consequential, and occasionally emotion-laden social judgements and action situations. And teachers' implicit theories about themselves and their work are thought to play an important part in the judgements and interpretations that teachers make every day.

As the term *implicit theory* implies, these systems of thought are not clearly articulated or codified by their owners, but are typically inferred and reconstructed by researchers on teacher thinking. The study of implicit theories employs various methods including stimulated recall interviews, linguistic analysis of teacher talk, paragraph completion tests, responses to simulation materials such as vignettes describing hypothetical students or classroom situations, and concept generation and mapping exercises such as the Kelly Repertory Grid Technique. Research designs also vary considerably from ethnographic case studies of one or two teachers (Elbaz, 1981; Kroma, 1983; Clandinin, 1986) to standardized administration of a belief inventory, judgement task, or stimulated recall protocol to several teachers (e.g. Conners, 1978; Marland, 1977; Munby, 1983). Variability in researchers' methods, designs, contexts and interpretive frames of reference leads to great variability in how teachers' implicit theories are described. Some recent research by Berliner and Carter (1986) has begun to examine how implicit theories develop over time, by describing and contrasting the perceptions of veteran teachers with those of beginners.

Leaving teachers and their implicit theories for a moment, let us consider research that is primarily about students learning science. Studies of the teaching and learning of science (e.g. Roth, Smith and Anderson, 1983; Roth, 1985) indicate that students come to a science lesson or course with preconceptions about the phenomena and processes in the science curriculum. For example, fifth graders (10-year-olds) come to a lesson on photosynthesis with their own ideas about how plants get nourishment or to a physics unit on light and vision with preconceptions about how we see. Often, these preconceptions are incomplete, flawed and in conflict with currently accepted scientific explanations. And almost always, students' preconceptions are robust, that is, students continue to hold and think from flawed but familiar preconceptions about the world even after having been taught scientifically correct explanations (Roth, 1985). Researchers advocating an approach to teaching called 'teaching for conceptual change' (Posner, Strike, Hewson and Gertzog, 1982; Roth, 1985) have demonstrated that students' preconceptions can be revised or replaced with scientifically correct conceptions only if considerable teaching time and energy are devoted to unmasking and incontrovertibly confronting students' misconceptions before proceeding with instruction.

Returning to the question posed above, what does a consultant who knows this research have to work with, in the service of teacher-educators? Teachers have implicit theories, students have preconceptions. Both are robust, idiosyncratic, sensitive to the particular experiences of the holder, incomplete, familiar and sufficiently pragmatic to have gotten the teacher or student to where they are today. Neither is likely to read like a textbook or to be quickly and thoroughly replaced by the usual lecture, reading, discussion, practice and evaluation methods typically employed in teacher preparation programmes. Implicit theories and preconceptions affect perception, interpretation, and judgement and therefore have potentially important consequences in what teachers and students do and say.

In the context of teacher education these claims and information about implicit theories and preconceptions have provocative implications. Students begin teacher education programmes with their own ideas and beliefs about what it takes to be a successful teacher. These preconceptions are formed from thousands of hours of observation of teachers, good and bad, over the previous 15 or so years. Undoubtedly, students' conceptions of teaching are incomplete, for they typically see and hear only the performance side of classroom teaching. With this in mind, a thoughtful teacher-educator might ask: What are the preconceptions about teaching and learning held by our students? How should we take account of what our students know and believe as we help them prepare to be teachers? How might we structure field observations early in a teacher preparation programme to make visible important aspects of teaching not usually obvious to primary school or high school students? What do prospective teachers believe about the integration of subject matter knowledge with pedagogical skills, and what does our preparation programme offer to support or challenge and replace these preconceptions? These are not questions to which research on teacher thinking offers answers. Rather, these are potentially useful questions that might not otherwise have been asked in the absence of research on teacher thinking.

Beyond pursuing answers to questions about prospective teachers, this research can stimulate introspective questions about teacher-educators themselves. What do we as teacher-educators believe about teaching and learning, individually and as a group? How consistent are our espoused beliefs with our methods of teaching and evaluation (that is, do we practise what we preach)? Are the implicit and explicit theories of teacher-educators who supervise practice teaching likely to dominate and wash out what has been taught earlier in a teacher preparation programme? How does variability in implicit theories among supervisors of practice teaching influence and bias their judgements and evaluations of our students? Asking questions like these has led a number of teacher-educators to take the risky and exciting step of systematically studying their own practices. For example, several studies of the influence of implicit theories and belief systems of clinical supervisors on their judgements of student teachers have been completed in the last few years (Niemeyer and Moon, 1986; Rust, 1986). These studies have contributed to deliberation about who should be doing clinical observations (i.e. Should this usually low-status task be delegated to inexperienced graduate assistants, to experienced teachers hired for these purposes, to experienced teacher-educators, experts in the academic disciplines, or teams from two or three of these groups?), how clinical observations should be done, what kinds of evidence might be used in student teacher evaluation, and how clinical supervisors might prepare themselves for their important and demanding work. This research has also begun to contribute to an enhanced sense of professional identity among teacher-educators who specialize in clinical supervision, insofar as it has demonstrated the complexity and intellectual demands of this aspect of teacher education and drawn attention to the potentially pivotal role of the clinical supervisor in the process of teacher preparation.

PLANNING AND REFLECTION

Research on teacher planning consists of a score or more of studies every bit as variable in method and design as the work on implicit theories. Two distinctive features, however, set planning apart from implicit theories. First, virtually everyone involved with education agrees that planning is a real phenomenon, that is, all teachers do something they call planning at some time. And second, many now see teacher planning as the instrumental linking process between curriculum on the one hand and the particulars of instruction on the other. Psychologically, to understand teacher planning is to understand how teachers transform and interpret knowledge, formulate intentions and act from that knowledge and those intentions. From the curriculum theorist's point of view, the study of teacher planning can help explain why and how curriculum materials are understood or misunderstood, used, distorted, ignored, or transcended in classroom instruction. Politically and administratively, to control teacher planning is to control, in large measure, the content, pace, emphasis and process of instruction. And, from the practising teacher's point of view, the study of teacher planning can enhance appreciation of the genuinely professional (as distinct from technical) aspects of teaching. That is, the study of teacher planning documents the many ways in which the practice of teaching is as complex and demanding as the practice of medicine, law, or architecture.

Those who began to do research on teacher planning 10 or 15 years ago did not anticipate that this work had potential for being so central to the concerns of so many audiences. It has only been in hindsight that teacher thinking researchers have come to believe that to understand teacher planning is to understand much of teaching; that the study of how teachers prepare for instruction reveals a great deal about which features of subject matter, students, and of the physical, psychological, administrative, and political environments actually influence classroom instruction. One can theorize with the best of intentions about how teaching and school learning could be optimized, but the finest ideas and proposals must still pass through the funnel of teacher planning.

Research on teacher thinking has made modest but suggestive beginnings in the study of teacher planning. It has been established that experienced teachers do several different types of planning in the course of the school year (Clark and Yinger, 1979), that the time-honoured rational model (moving from learning objectives, through generating alternatives, to choice of an optimal alternative) is not used regularly by experienced teachers (Morine-Dershimer and Vallance, 1976; Yinger, 1977), although experienced teachers do claim that the rational model ought to be taught to novices (Neale, Pace and Case, 1983). Teachers do attend to learning outcomes, sometimes prior to teaching (while planning), sometimes during teaching, and sometimes only after interactive teaching is over (McLeod, 1981). Teachers also attend to goals, issues and concerns other than learning outcomes in their planning. And the teacher planning process serves immediate personal purposes for teachers, such as study of content, anxiety reduction and confidence building, as well as longer range instrumental purposes, determining the content and structure of classroom interaction (Carnahan, 1980; Hill, Yinger and Robbins, 1981; Peterson, Marx and Clark, 1978).

Psychological models of the planning process have been proposed and, to some degree, tested against the realities of practice (e.g. Clark and Yinger, 1979; Yinger, 1977). And styles of planning used by experienced teachers such as 'incremental planning' (Clark and Yinger, 1979) have been described. Curriculum planning has been shown to vary with the subject matter under consideration and with the degree of novelty or familiarity of the material, students and teaching setting (Clark and Elmore, 1981). North American primary school teachers report spending relatively large amounts of time planning (10 to 20 hours per week), but also report that relatively little time or support for planning is officially sanctioned or encouraged (Clark and Yinger, 1979). An

important product of the planning process is routines (Yinger, 1979) or structured patterns of teacher and student behaviour. The first weeks of the school
year have been shown to be a particularly important period for teacher planning,
inasmuch as many of the routines, rules, relationships and expectations that
influence classroom interaction during the remainder of the year are planned,
negotiated, replanned, and established during that time (Anderson and Evertson, 1978; Buckley and Cooper, 1978; Clark and Elmore, 1979; Shultz and Florio,
1979; Tikunoff and Ward, 1978).

One of the side effects of doing research on teacher thinking has been the
discovery and elaboration of techniques and procedures for promoting reflection
and analysis by teachers of their own thinking and behaviour. These techniques
include journal keeping, clinical interviewing, stimulated recall procedures in
which teachers view videotaped recordings (or sometimes listen to audiotapes) of
their teaching and respond to questions about their thinking, perceptions,
decisions and intentions, and concept generation and conceptual mapping tasks.
To study teacher thinking, researchers must depend on teachers to think aloud,
either while in the act of thinking and deciding, or retrospectively; one cannot
observe thought directly.

Hand in glove with these technical developments is the evolution of a
commitment to including teachers themselves as full partners in the study of
teacher thinking. To some degree, this change in the role that teachers play in the
research process from experimental subject to colleague and collaborator follows
from the invisible nature of teacher thinking and from the model role of the
'informant' in ethnographic studies of societies linguistically and culturally
different from that of the anthropologist. And, in part, the enhanced role of
teachers in research on teacher thinking reflects ideological and political commit-
ments to share power more equitably between the communities of research and of
practice. In any case, teachers have found themselves thinking aloud, reflecting,
raising and refining questions about their knowledge and practice, writing,
analysing data, making formal presentations of research in which they have been
involved, and publishing for audiences of researchers and teachers. A great deal
of this has happened due largely to the advent of research on teacher thinking
(Porter, 1986).

A recurring theme in conversations between researchers and teachers collaborating in these ways concerns the powerful effects on teachers of reflecting on
their own practice. Experienced teachers report that describing their plans and
intentions, explaining their reasons underlying action and decision, and responding to the questions and presence of an informed, non-judgemental adult
seem to breathe new life and meaning into their teaching. Usually, teaching is an
action-oriented, operational profession. But the intervention of researchers
describing planning, thinking, and decision-making has required that teachers
stop and think, find words and reasons for their thoughts and beliefs, and take a
second look at themselves and their teaching. While not intended by the
researchers as professional development activities, the journal keeping, clinical

interviews, stimulated recall sessions, and articulation of beliefs and implicit principles of practice have instigated a new awareness among a few teachers. These techniques and the genuine human interest in understanding that accompany their use may constitute professional development activities of the broadest kind. That is, they may enable teachers to see and appreciate what is genuinely professional about their work; to kindle or revive the idealism, freshness, and commitment to self-improvement that we often see in the best first-year teachers, but this time, with a difference: the difference that years of accumulated practical wisdom brings. In sum, reflection by teachers makes a difference, albeit a difference expressed in many different ways.

What does this mix of fact, theory and opinion about teacher planning and reflection offer to a consultant, trying to be helpful to teacher-educators? He or she might bring questions like these to deliberations about teacher preparation: when and how do prospective teachers learn about and practice planning? How many kinds of planning do they practise? To what extent does their practice planning take account of the structural and practical differences between school subject matters (e.g. the concept of 'guided practice' may be realized in quite different ways in the contexts of essay writing or maths problem solving)? Is the theory and practice of planning as expressed in university courses consistent with the procedures and criteria for successful planning built into the practice teaching experience? What do our approaches to training teachers to plan reveal about our implicit theories of teaching (e.g. teaching as literal implementation of curriculum materials, teaching as imitation of experienced models, teaching as curriculum building and adaptation, teaching as behaviour management)? If planning during the first days and weeks of the school year is so important, do our prospective teachers ever get to see and participate in this kind of planning? To what extent do our teacher education students have opportunities to plan, teach, re-plan, and re-teach, thus learning about the limits of foresight and about improvement-orientated self-observation? Do we include techniques and opportunities for reflection and professional communication among teachers in our training programmes? And how do we, the teacher-educators, show that we value and practise reflection and self-examination about our own teaching? Again, the researcher-consultant brings no crisp and prescriptive answers to these questions. But they are questions worth pursuing, and the pursuit must be framed by the all-important context of particular professional preparation programmes. Teacher planning and reflection are not the whole of teaching, but research on teacher thinking suggests that they deserve explicit and creative attention throughout a sound teacher education programme.

DILEMMAS AND UNCERTAINTY

The third set of contributions of research on teacher thinking to discourse about teacher preparation concerns the very nature of the teaching situation itself. Not 'what works', but 'what it is really like out there', as seen through the eyes of teachers themselves. In three words, teaching as experienced is *complex, uncertain* and peppered with *dilemmas*.

The research on teacher planning alluded to above speaks eloquently to the complexity and uncertainty inherent in interactive teaching. Indeed, a great deal of teachers' planning energy goes into trying to predict and anticipate potential problems, to guess and estimate what students already know and how they might respond, and to forming plans and routines that are robust to the interruptions and distractions that assault most teachers most of the time.

Researchers have also studied the thinking and decision-making that teachers do during the act of teaching. This research has explored the extent to which teachers make on-the-spot decisions that change their plans or behaviour in the classroom, and attempted to identify the cues used by teachers in reaching these interactive decisions. A few studies have explored the relationships between patterns of interactive decision-making and student achievement, and some compare thinking processes of experts with those of novices in the same situations. Like the literature on teaching planning, the number of studies available is small, and the teachers studied are mostly experienced primary school teachers.

Research on interactive decision-making indicates that teachers encounter decision situations at two-minute intervals while teaching – literally hundreds of decision points per day. This research also indicates that the greatest proportion of teachers' interactive thoughts is about students (between 39 per cent and 50 per cent), followed by instructional behaviour and procedures, content, materials and learning objectives (Peterson and Clark, 1978). Marland (1977) categorized teachers' interactive thoughts as perceptions, interpretations, anticipations and reflections. There is some evidence to support the idea that teachers consider improvising major changes in instructional process primarily when their teaching is going poorly, that is, when the myriad adjustments and small changes that teachers make in the ongoing classroom process prove insufficient in maintaining the flow of the lesson (Peterson and Clark, 1978). This is consistent with findings from studies of the cognitive processing of professionals in other fields who are described by Simon (1957) as pursuing a strategy of 'Satisficing' rather than optimizing. Research by Doyle (1979) also indicates that it is 'adaptive and efficient for a teacher to direct conscious processing primarily to discrepancies or anomalies. By specializing in discrepancies, a teacher can anticipate disruptions and reduce the effects of immediacy and unpredictability on task accomplishment' (Doyle, 1979, pp. 62–63).

Leinhardt and Greeno (1984) describe the cognitive structures that teachers use to move back and forth between implementing pre-planned routines and adjusting their actions to new information that becomes available in the course of a lesson. They found experienced teachers to be distinguished by their ability to obtain and retain new information in interaction with students while continuing to maintain control of their agenda. Others have compared the schema that experienced teachers use to understand what is happening in the classroom with the way novices understand the same situation (Berliner and Carter, 1986; Calderhead, 1983; Housner and Griffey, 1983).

Three studies examined the relationship between interactive decision making and student on-task behaviour or achievement (Doyle, 1977; Morine and Vallance, 1974; Peterson, Marx and Clark, 1978). The interactive decision-making of effective teachers is characterized by rapid judgement, 'chunking' of many events and cues into a few categories, differentiation of cues and events as to their importance, and a willingness to change the course of classroom inter-action when necessary.

These studies of teacher planning and decision-making tell us a great deal about the task demands of teaching as well as about how particular teachers cope with those demands. The task environment of the classroom has been charac-terized by Shulman (1984) as more complex than that faced by a physician in a diagnostic examination. This complexity has been described by Clark and Lamp-ert (1986) as follows:

> The teacher encounters a host of interrelated and competing decision situations both while planning and during teaching. There are no perfect or optimal solutions to these decisions. A gain for one student or in one subject matter may mean a foregone opportunity for others. A motivationally and intellectually profitable digression may reduce time devoted to the mandated curriculum. Such conflicts among teachers' multiple commitments lead to practical dilemmas (Berlak and Berlak, 1981; Lampert, 1984) which must be managed in interaction with students. Conflicting goals, combined with endemic uncertainty about how to achieve desired outcomes can lead to 'knots' in teachers' thinking (Wagner, 1984). Often these entanglements can only be sorted out as the teacher experiments with action and observes its outcomes (Lampert, 1985). By such experimentation, teachers build a store of personal practical knowledge about how to get their job done (Clandinin and Connelly, 1984). (p. 28)

In sum, research on teacher thinking has made an empirical case that the practice of teaching is complex, uncertain, and dilemma-riddled. And this research has described how some teachers see, feel, and cope with the greyness. What questions might a hypothetical consultant raise with teacher-educators that follow from seeing teaching thus? First, one might ask how thoroughly and persuasively a teacher preparation programme informs its postulants that there is more to teaching than meets the eye; that expertise in teaching is less a matter of knowing all the answers than a matter of making the most of the unexpected. While the system of education in China supports the role of the teacher as a virtuoso who creates, practises and polishes exquisitely set pieces of pedagogical performance (Paine, 1986), the teacher in North American schools is faced with a mind-boggling array of mutually incompatible expectations and imperatives. Do prospective teachers hear this, come to believe this, and take it into account in forming their emergent expectations and implicit theories? Do methods courses, micro-teaching, and other preparatory experiences reflect the intrinsic uncertainty of teaching? Or do teacher education programmes control, oversimplify and distort practice teaching and field observation experiences to such a degree that our students' practice time is wasted or misdirected in irrelevant and unrepresentative test-like activities? Do the teachers of teachers have the courage to think aloud as they themselves wrestle with troubling dilemmas such as striking a balance between depth and breadth of content studied, distribution of time and attention among individual students, making inferences about what students know and what marks they should be assigned, or with how to repair errors, teaching disasters, and the human mistakes that even experienced teacher-educators make from time to time? Do we claim to be graduating fully-functioning teachers or novices well-started? How might teacher preparation programmes be sowing the seeds of learned helplessness and incompetence by advocating practices that simply do not work for novices? For example, teacher-educators in two otherwise exemplary preparation programmes (studied by Ball and Feiman-Nemser, 1986) taught their students that good teachers don't use published textbooks or basal readers, they create their own materials. This well-intentioned advice set up students for failure and embarrassment during practice teaching because the teacher preparation programmes did not equip these beginners to create original materials of high quality and practicality, and because their experienced cooperating teachers typically relied on textbooks and basal readers quite heavily. Here we have a case of unintentional sabotage of a potentially crucial learning experience.

Research on teacher thinking does not promise to discover a generically effective method or set of techniques for dealing with uncertainty, complexity, or dilemmas. By their very natures these qualities defy the quest for a technical fix. However, the teacher-educator who abandons the fiction that teaching can become a technically exact scientific enterprise, and who has the courage to reveal how he or she agonizes over real dilemmas and contradictions – that teacher-educator is likely to be successful at helping prospective teachers to prepare themselves for uncertainty. That teacher-educator is likely to minimize the boredom and burnout that plague the profession. That teacher-educator is asking the right questions about teacher preparation.

CONCLUSION

Teacher preparation is already being affected, to some degree, by research on teacher thinking, Thoughtful teacher-educators are learning about this research, thinking from it, and asking questions about the ways in which they help their students become well-started and thoughtful novice teachers.

Research on teacher thinking has helped us to appreciate in some detail the complexity, artistry and demands of classroom teaching. And this work now serves as rich food for thought (and action) for colleagues who have chosen the challenging work of influencing the knowledge, skills and dispositions of those who would teach. There are reasons to hope that this great conversation will broaden and continue, with researchers, teacher-educators and those who play both roles pursuing answers to a final question: how can we help our students to *prepare themselves* to think and act in ways that will eventually become good teaching?

Chapter 13

Teachers as Designers in Self-Directed Professional Development

In some quarters the phrase 'professional development of teachers' carries a great deal of negative baggage. It implies: a process done to teachers; that teachers need to be forced into developing; that teachers have deficits in knowledge and skill that can be fixed by training; and that teachers are pretty much alike. Now, as a teacher, how eager would you feel about cooperating in a process in which you are presumed to be passive, resistant, deficient and one of a faceless, homogeneous herd? This is hardly an ideal set of conditions for adult learning, support, and development.

The good news is that teachers are not passive, needy, deficient, and homogeneous. We know this from personal experience and from research. Research on teacher thinking, which began in earnest in 1976, supports and describes the experienced professional teacher as a complex individual doing very complicated work in a sometimes stressful, sometimes rewarding, always uncertain and dynamic variety of settings.

Research on teacher thinking is only one source of information about the nature of teaching, and it is the source that I will draw on most heavily here. My simple message has three parts: 1) there is much more to teaching than meets the eye; 2) the enriched image of teachers as reflective professionals is a good place to start in rethinking professional development; and 3) experienced teachers can become designers of their own personal programmes of self-directed professional development. First, let us examine what researchers on teacher thinking have discovered and concluded about teachers and teaching.

My review and summary of research on teacher thinking (Clark and Peterson, 1986), summarized about 10 years of research on topics such as teacher planning, interactive decision-making, judgement and implicit theories. This work broke new ground in that, for the first time, educational researchers chose to rely on teachers to think aloud, describe their thoughts and decision processes, and make the invisible aspects of teaching visible. In short, teachers were taken seriously as professionals as a starting condition for this research. Teachers rose to this long overdue occasion. The image of the teacher that emerges from this research is far more flattering and complex than was the case 10 or 12 years ago.

The teacher as an intelligent, reflective professional was not invented by researchers on teaching, but this image was given new credence and support.

In sum, research on teacher thinking supports the position that teachers are more active than passive, more ready to learn than resistant, more wise and knowledgeable than deficient, and more diverse and unique than they are homogeneous. This is a flattering and optimistic picture, and it is not true of all teachers in all situations. But it is true often enough to be taken seriously, as a point of departure for asking 'What can we do to make professional development programmes work for professional teachers?' The answer is deceptively simple: we must give the responsibility for professional development to teachers themselves. This is what I mean by 'Self- Directed Professional Development'.

Why should teachers, individually and collectively, take charge of their own professional development? Why is this a good idea? First, we need to recognize that adult development is voluntary – no one can force a person to learn, change or grow. When adults feel that they are in control of a process of change that they have voluntarily chosen, they are much more likely to realize full value from it than when coerced into training situations in which they have little say about the timing, the process, or the goals. Second, because each teacher is unique in important ways, it is impossible to create a single, centrally administered and planned programme of professional development that will meet everyone's needs and desires. Why not let the individual be in charge of asking and answering the timeless questions: 'Who am I? What do I need? How can I get help?' Third, I advocate self-directed professional development because I think that is the way that the best teachers already operate. Wouldn't it be good for all teachers to have support and encouragement for following an approach to lifelong learning that is pursued now only by a few crusty and inspiring veterans? I think so.

To summarize the argument to this point: there is more to teaching than meets the eye, and responsibility for teachers' professional development ought to be placed in the hands of teachers themselves. Building on these two propositions, there is one more level to detail to address about the idea of self-directed professional development. To carry off the concept of self-directed professional development, we, as teachers, must begin to think of ourselves as designers. To develop ourselves as professionals, we must plan, select, sketch, make errors and rearrange the familiar furniture of the mind. We must design ourselves, and continue to revise, redesign and learn from experience. We must conspire with the world to make for ourselves a heaven or purgatory of our own designing.

The idea of teachers as designers of their own professional development is a metaphor that can become real. To form a picture of what it means to be a designer, think of the different examples of design professions that you already know something about: interior design, architecture, consumer product design, urban planning, filmmaking, advertising, menu planning, sculpture, photography, music composition and cosmetology, to name a few. You can add others to this list, to persuade yourself that you already know a good bit about design, in its many varieties, and that you already are acting as a designer in some domains.

The question is not whether teachers have what it takes to be designers of their own professional development. They do. The question is, How can we help with the process? My tentative answer is to offer and illustrate a list of seven principles of design that I hope will help those teachers who choose to take on this responsibility.

PRINCIPLES OF DESIGN

1. Write Your Own Credo of Teaching

What a teacher knows and believes about teaching, about learning, about curriculum, and about self and his or her students is quite important to professional development. Our beliefs and personal theories set boundaries or frames around what we see and how we interpret experience. Our attention is selective; we can't attend to everything. And our beliefs and theories define what is foreground and what is background; what to attend to and what to ignore.

By itself, this process of seeing the world through our own theoretical lenses is no problem. It is simply the way that people deal with complex situations. But it can become a problem for a professional teacher when this interpretive process and the beliefs and theories that underlie it remain completely unconscious. In this case, we become mechanical, reactionary, bored and frustrated. The implicit theories that once were tools for thoughtful interpretation become tyrants, manipulating us in painfully familiar patterns.

Teachers' implicit theories are more than private matters of personal taste and opinion. They can have dramatic consequences. For example, consider a study of kindergarten teachers published by researchers Mary Lee Smith and Lorrie Shepard (1988). They were commissioned to help the administration in a school district understand the causes and consequences of radically different patterns of retaining children, that is, having children repeat the kindergarten year. They interviewed 40 of the 44 teachers of kindergarten in the district to find out, among other things, what each teacher believed about children and how they develop, learn, and adapt to the changing demands of schooling. The researchers found two broad belief patterns in the teachers' responses: a 'nativist' belief system, in which only the passage of time can enable child development, and three 'non-nativist' theories, in which child development is believed to be affected by teaching, encouragment, family support and other factors in addition to maturation. In short, the researchers found that both sides of the classic 'nature vs. nurture' debate are represented among these kindergarten teachers.

Now, if this were all that Smith and Shepard had discovered – if they had stopped with description of two kinds of implicit theories held by teachers – I would be interested but not alarmed. But the researchers went farther, to correlate beliefs with actions, and found that the nativist teachers retained children for a second year of kindergarten much more frequently than did teachers who held non-nativist positions. Retention rates varied from a low of 1 per cent to a high of 25 per cent. In other words, a child's chances of spending two years in kindergarten depend, to a significant degree, on a teacher's implicit theory of child development. Implicit theories can make a difference. Implicit beliefs have consequences.

Returning to the first principle of design, what I am advocating here is that we resolve to wake up, to take our own beliefs and implicit theories seriously, and to make them more explicit and visible, at least to ourselves. Beliefs and theories that remain unconscious and implicit will not grow or become elaborated, or evolve in response to critical analysis. For our beliefs and theories to develop, we must get them out on the table where we can see them. So, I recommend that you spell out what you know and believe about teaching, in writing, once a year. Do it in the spring, or on a summer holiday, or on your birthday. You'll be surprised at some of what you write, and gratified by the ways in which your story changes over the years. And seeing your statement of belief, your own credo of teaching, will alert you to topics and questions helpful in designing your personal course of professional development.

2. Start With Your Strengths

One reason that traditional professional development has negative overtones is that most of the time it is designed to focus on and fix up our weaknesses. It is grounded in a disease model. Professional developers promise a quick fix for our deficits, if only we will cooperate in our humiliation and redemption. The problem with this, of course, is that professionals are not interested in being humiliated as a prerequisite to learning and development. That approach simply doesn't work.

Even seasoned and gifted teachers can fall into deficit model thinking. I was privileged to attend an English Department staff meeting at an outstanding secondary school in California. The agenda was to plan professional development activities for themselves. They had a generous budget. They were free to bring in outside experts in their fields. There were no administrators present. It seemed like all the conditions were in place for a wonderful, positive exercise in self-directed professional development. But the meeting got into a downward spiral from the start. All of the suggestions for consultants and activities were tied to perceived weaknesses in their programme. Enthusiasm trailed off. If this was what professional development was going to mean this year, no one wanted a big dose of it.

After listening to this for 30 minutes, I made the suggestion that the staff list the things that they did particularly well and were proud of in their English programme and proud of about their students. Then, we re-framed the planning problem as 'How can we build on, show off and celebrate the many things we already do well?' I'm happy to report that this changed the whole tone of the meeting, for the better. Now everyone has ideas for inviting experts, organizing conferences, and for involving their students, colleagues from other departments, and staff from a nearby university in their professional development plan. There was a real charge in the air when the bell rang – no one wanted the meeting to end. This was a group excited about shaping their own professional development.

So, what might we conclude from this experience? Professional teachers need to let go of the idea that we have the responsibility to become excellent at everything. Instead, make an inventory of the ways of teaching that you do well and that are close to your heart. Then, choose professional development activities that help you celebrate, improve and show off the things you love to do. Give yourself permission to lead with your strengths.

3. Make a Five-Year Plan

You've heard it said many times: 'If you don't know where you are going, you'll never get there.' I prefer the Arabic version which goes: 'To the traveller with no destination, one road is as good as another.' I prefer this second version of wisdom because it warns me of a trap. A life, a career, or a journey full of motion can still be aimless and empty. Meaning and a sense of direction and progress don't come automatically from activity, even apparently competent activity. A professional career made up of doing what we guess other people expect of us can lead to a painful and sometimes tragic mid-career crisis.

To some extent, a mid-career reassessment is part of normal human development. Adults tend to ask different questions of themselves and their work at different ages. Remember your first year or two of teaching? The big questions were: 'Will I make it? Can I survive? Was this a big mistake?' Later, you came to believe that you finally knew something and were doing pretty well. For me, this stage lasted about six weeks. Then I turned 40. I began to ask, 'Is this all there is? Is this as good as it gets? Have I painted myself into a corner, using paint that takes 25 years to dry?'

Especially at this mid-career time, taking charge of your own plan for professional development can be a life-saver. When the world itself and the structure of the profession cease to give a sense of growth and progress, you can begin to provide that for yourself. Sketch the ways in which you hope to be different four or five years from now, and some of the possible means to those changes. Recognize that some of the most important developmental changes involve doing less (e.g. less yelling, less testing, less worrying), rather than always adding more knowledge, skill, or activity.

Of course, this five-year plan should not be allowed to completely dominate our lives and choices. In studying the instructional planning of teachers, I've learned at least two things: that it is important to have a plan, and that it is important to feel free to depart from the plan when reality does not match our predictions. A plan can give us direction, a way to begin, a feeling of control, and a basis for evaluating our choices. But a plan is not a script.

4. Look in Your Own Backyard

One of the facts of life for teachers is that, no matter how enlightened your school authorities may be about professional development, you will spend between 170 and 190 days of the school year in your own classroom. This is not likely to change in the foreseeable future, except in the direction of a longer school year. And that is fine with most teachers – the classroom is where we belong. The challenge of this fourth principle of design is to figure out ways to make a virtue of the fact that teachers can rarely go elsewhere in search of professional development support. How can we continue to nurture our own professional development in our own backyards?

Anthropologists who study teaching and learning have coined an expression that may be helpful with this challenge. They say that, in order to appreciate the richness and complexity of familiar everyday situations, we must 'make the familiar strange'. This involves at least two steps: first, to believe that interesting, exciting, amazing things are happening all around us all the time, and, second, to become a questioner of the traditional ways and reasons and explanations that we usually take for granted. Try to see the 'taken for granted' through the eyes of a novice teacher or of a Martian. Experiment by reversing the order in which you do things (e.g. give the final exam at the beginning of a unit, or on Tuesday instead of Friday). Exchange roles by having students become teachers while you become the student. All the while, pay attention to what you are learning about yourself, your students, about subject matter, and about the ways that your usual classroom organization works to make some things possible and others difficult. This approach can be a powerful antidote to the feeling of being trapped in a boring and completely predictable job.

One example of discovering the amazing within the apparently ordinary happened for me in October 1987. I was working as a teacher's aide in a second grade (7-year-olds) classroom as part of my role as Professor In Residence at Whitehills Elementary School. The teacher and the children were making apple sauce that afternoon and also writing about the process. I helped by supervising the apple peeling and cutting, the clean-up, and the tasting. And I also wrote a short piece describing that afternoon and attempting to answer the question 'What can you learn from making apple sauce?' (see Part Three). I was surprised and gratified to discover that there is a great deal that can be learned from making apple sauce. And the teacher herself was surprised by how much there was to this activity, once she stopped to think about it. The answers came tumbling over one another, as soon as the question was put. And this is the point: if we ask real questions about the everyday events of our ordinary lives, we'll more often than not be amazed and delighted with how much we can learn in our own backyards.

5. Ask for Support

On the one hand, each teacher's path and pattern of development is a solitary journey. I advocate that we accept this, take responsibility for our own development, and make the most of it. On the other hand, there is no rule that requires us to pursue this solitary journey without any outside help. The paradox is that becoming a fully developed autonomous and thoughtful individual is a process that we can't do alone.

Asking for help is often difficult for us teachers, for most of us have succeeded by being rugged individualists, by keeping our eyes on our own papers and by choosing to try only those activities in which we are pretty confident of immediate success. We want to look good all of the time. Asking for help makes us feel vulnerable – vulnerable to being discovered as imposters who don't know as much as we pretend to know. The words 'I have a problem' become 'I am a problem'.

But the simple truth is that we each need help and support. Most educators love to give help, if only we would ask. A friend of mine who teaches third grade (8-year-olds) was in a real bind one autumn. She agreed to the installation of two nice micro-computer systems in her classroom. But she did not have a clue about how to make use of them, nor did she have any inclination to become a computer whiz herself. But there was the hardware, staring back at her and the third graders. And there were parental and administration expectations to deal with. She solved her problem in an elegant way, by asking for help, from fourth graders. The teacher realized that some students in the school already had more expertise than most adults in the use of micro-computers. Risky as it felt to turn over a measure of control to the children, she did so. Beyond solving an immediate practical problem for the teacher, this sequence of events opened her eyes to other ways in which seeing 'kids as experts' can change the whole learning environment for the better.

Other forms of help include time, money, equipment, ideas, encouragement and appreciation. Asking for help does not guarantee that it will be delivered. But not asking for help virtually guarantees that you will remain helpless.

6. Go First Class

As a professional teacher, you deserve respect. And that begins with respecting yourself. If we think and act like second class citizens, like we deserve to be treated as doormats, there are plenty of people who will oblige us. And as we treat ourselves with respect, our students, our colleagues, our administrative helpers and the public will begin to do likewise. At the very least, we will begin to teach by example how to treat teachers more respectfully.

Learning to treat oneself with respect can be a life's work. It involves accepting both my successes and my failures, my bright side and my shadow side, and believing that I am intrinsically worthwhile and lovable, regardless of whether I have done enough good works to earn love and appreciation. Coming to this position usually takes more than a two-day workshop on building self-esteem.

But there are some relatively direct ways to express our self-respect in support of our own professional development. Read great literature, visit Stratford and take in a play, use the most beautiful room available for your conference, buy yourself a beautiful pen, make an art of your professional development and practise showing sincere respect for others, children and adults alike. For there is a part of the human mind that experiences the way we treat others as directed towards ourselves.

For five summers I was a staff member at a workshop for secondary school teachers held at Stanford University. There were many factors that contributed to the success of this ten-day programme. But I want to focus on one: we met in the most handsomely appointed conference room on campus. The room is located on the top floor of the Aeronautics and Astronautics Building, is very comfortably furnished, and opens on to a big, sunny balcony overlooking the red tile roofs and palm trees of a beautiful campus. From the first moment of the workshop, a message is clear: teachers are important people who ought to be treated in a first-class manner.

7. Blow Your Own Horn

My final suggestion for a principle of design is to blow your own horn. Let others know what you are doing on your own behalf and how good you feel about yourself. Learn how to teach about what you are learning. Teach about what excites you. Exaggerate during your annual review. Make a demonstration videotape, or write a paper, or invite a fellow teacher to visit your class, or report once a year at a staff meeting.

These may sound like difficult things to do for humble, self-effacing teachers like us, and they are. But the real benefits of blowing your own horn have nothing to do with taking credit from others or showing off. The real benefits come from confronting and answering difficult questions like: 'What have I been doing lately that is worthwhile and interesting? What ideas and insights have I had that might be useful to others? How do I want to frame and remember the positive side of this year?' Blowing your own horn is the means for making coherent and public the ways in which your professional development is developing.

CONCLUSION

In conclusion, I hope that this line of argument, moving from research on teacher thinking to self-directed professional development, to principles of design, has provoked your thinking. This has been the story of how I am trying to organize and make sense of my own professional development. Each of you has made your own sense of this story. If my words have confirmed what some of you already know and are doing, have puzzled some, enraged others, and gotten the germ of an idea started, then I have succeeded, and so have you. May you all continue to develop as professionals, each in your own way.

Chapter 14

Veteran Teachers Learning With Beginners

If the literature and folklore of learning to teach agree on one point, it is that student teaching or practicum is important. Clearly, researchers on teacher education have found the practicum a frequent and interesting focus for inquiry. As well, it is commonplace in the oral tradition of teacher education for recent graduates and experienced teachers alike to nominate their student teaching as the time 'When I really learned to teach', or even as 'The only practical and worthwhile part of my teacher preparation'. Virtually everyone who is now or once was a teacher can recall at least one telling story about student teaching. It is a milestone experience whose scars and laurels stay with us for life.

Scholars have studied student teaching empirically and analysed its role philosophically and sociologically, and even psychodynamically. Almost unanimously, researchers studying student teaching take the position that it is primarily a pedagogical encounter aimed at changing and evaluating the teacher candidate: changing and consolidating his or her skills, strategies, knowledge and dispositions. Studies of models of clinical supervision, of the nature, timing and duration of field experiences, of the interpersonal dynamics in the triad of student teacher, cooperating teacher and university supervisor, and studies of developmental shifts in concerns and expectations during student teaching – all these focus ultimately on the question 'How is the student teacher different as a consequence of these experiences?'

This is a fine question, worth pursuing. It is one of those perennial questions that deserves to be asked again and again, as the contexts and the forms of teacher education change. But it is not the question pursued here. Instead, I want to invite your attention to the neglected member of the field experience triad: the cooperating teacher. For it seems that just as parents are changed by raising their children, just as teachers are changed by their encounters with pupils, as a host family is changed by the foreign student guest in their home, and therapists by conversations with their clients, so too cooperating teachers must be influenced by student teachers. If thousands of experienced teachers *are* being influenced each year by student teachers in incidental and unsystematic ways, can or should teacher-educators do better by becoming more intentional about it?

What *do* veteran teachers learn from beginners, and how can that help with cultivating thoughtful teaching?

I do not have complete answers to these good questions, but I do have a collection of stories, ideas and testimonials offered by North American teachers in response to my asking 'What have you learned from working with a beginner learning to teach?' I hope that sharing some of their answers will inspire some to think and act on the idea that student teaching can be a form of professional development for the cooperating teacher.

Before I tell you what teachers have told me about their learning from beginners, I want to be more specific about what I mean by learning. Usually, we use the word 'learning' to refer to acquiring *new* information, knowledge, skills or dispositions through study, instruction, or practice. In thinking about what veteran teachers learn from beginners I want to include this conventional sense of learning and also go beyond it. I want to broaden the meaning of learning in this context to include the process of remembering, of *being reminded* of what one already knew, but with which one had lost touch. For, as you will see, this second sense of learning is quite prominent and arguably consequential in the mentor relationship. A veteran is less likely to change in response to novel information than as a consequence of re-thinking, remembering, and reorganizing what he or she already knows and believes.

With this expanded notion of learning in mind, I have organized teachers' reports of what they learn about from beginners into four categories:

1. Knowledge and Information
2. Time
3. Energy and Morale
4. Analysis of Teaching.

KNOWLEDGE AND INFORMATION

I once met a medical educator who had studied the dynamics of field experiences called 'clerkships', in which third- and fourth-year medical students work for eight or 10 weeks under the supervision of a practising physician. One of the benefits claimed by the veteran doctors in this relationship is access to the latest in medical treatment information – the most current procedures used at the University Hospital. This knowledge and information came from the medical student, not from professional journals, which lag months or even years behind best practice, nor from pharmaceutical salesmen, who are biased in favour of their company's product line. In short, the medical student brings a genuine and valued expertise to the practicum, in the form of very current technical knowledge and information.

Sadly, I have not found this to be the case with student teaching – this is one of the many ways in which the analogy between teacher education and medical education fails. Most student teachers in our present undergraduate preparation programmes are young and inexperienced people who have studied education part-time for the past 12 to 18 months. They tend to feel overwhelmed by the demands and complexities of practice (as do medical students), but also feel that they have been given relatively little at the university in the form of new knowledge and information that will serve them well in the classroom. Veteran teachers, for the most part, believe that they have little or nothing to learn from these callow youths. I have even heard one teacher express resentment at the presumptiveness of a student teacher who claimed that he had an idea or two about how things might be done better.

But the picture is not all bleak with regard to knowledge and information learned by veteran teachers who work with beginners. One teacher of first grade (6-year-olds), curious about the technical terms used by her student teacher describing 'teaching maths for understanding', arranged for a meeting with the university supervisor and several other cooperating teachers to have these terms and concepts explained. The initiative for learning lay with the veteran teacher, following her curiosity and taking the beginner's language seriously. The information and knowledge lay with the university supervisor. And both the triggering event and the opportunity for released time for the veteran teacher were supplied by the student teacher.

A more systematic and intentional approach to providing information and knowledge to cooperating teachers characterizes some teacher preparation designs. In these programmes continuing long-term relationships are established between university staff and a corps of mentor teachers. Two or three times each term the programme staff organize seminars for the mentor teachers to ensure that the field experience is going smoothly and to inform the mentor teacher about what undergraduate beginners are learning and doing in their university courses. In at least one programme the mentors also receive copies of the written assignments prepared by the prospective teachers who are visiting their classrooms. In short, these veteran teachers are being brought into the fold as teacher-educators; becoming better informed about relatively new developments in teacher education (e.g. teaching for conceptual change, constructivism, pedagogical content knowledge, multi-ability group activities); and joining a face-to-face network of other veteran teachers who are dealing with similar issues in teaching and teacher education.

It is clear to me that the knowledge and information learned by veteran teachers in the cases described above would not have been available but for their status as cooperating teachers. By signing on to work with a beginner, they can connect with the best that a staff of education has to offer and the best that their fellow veteran teachers can give, intellectually, emotionally and practically. Agreeing to work with a novice can be a ticket to a postgraduate professional education that rivals any collection of graduate courses, and that is embedded in the authentic context of one's own school.

A final thought on knowledge and information: subject matter knowledge has never come up as a category of need or of learning in my conversations with veteran teachers. Perhaps the topic is too threatening. Certainly the beginners are seldom experts in subject matter to the degree that veterans would have much to learn from them. And the vast majority of teacher-educators have much more to say about process than about content and its interpretation. Yet I feel that deepening teachers' understanding of the subjects taught in school is one of the most urgent of professional development priorities. It does not seem to be happening spontaneously, but the time and circumstances seem ripe.

TIME

Working with a student teacher changes the way in which a veteran teacher spends time. In some ways, time slows down when working with a beginner. Planning and preparation routines that the veteran has perfected over the years, with all their shortcuts and taken-for-granted contingency plans, must be spelled out in excruciating detail for the eager but uncertain novice. University-required lesson plans and unit plans take the novice hours to create and take some time for the veteran to review. Coordinating with another adult presses the mentor to be explicit and specific about what is going to happen when – certainly more explicit than when working alone. And, because plans rarely come true in every literal detail, the veteran and novice alike are at risk of feeling ineffectual for not making things come out as agreed. So the slowing down of time and the demand for explicitness can be frustrating to the veteran who has grown comfortable with mentally revising plans while driving to school, drawing on memories of how things went last year, and improvising by departing from the plan when professional judgement so indicates.

But there are also ways in which working with a student teacher frees up time for the veteran. This typically happens during the second half of the period of student teaching, when the beginner takes over full responsibility for the class. The question of concern to us here is: what can veteran teachers do with the hours freed up in this way?

I have already mentioned the case in which student teachers served, in effect, as substitute (supply) teachers while their mentors met in a one-time seminar with a university teacher-educator. I have also seen cooperating teachers in the teachers' common room preparing report cards and struggling to write accurate, helpful and supportive comments about pupil progress while their student teachers are in charge down the hall. These teachers appreciated the opportunity to use 'company time' to better prepare themselves for parent conferences, to be a bit more reflective about student progress than they would have had time for otherwise, and to think ahead about ways to help learners who are not making hoped-for-progress.

Two other stories illustrate how cooperating teachers made creative use of time freed by student teachers. The first is of a male teacher of grade two (7-year-olds) in a K-6 (5- to 11-year-olds) school, who offered to teach one full day in each of the other six classrooms in his school. During the six-week period when his student teacher was soloing in grade two, he prepared for and taught a Tuesday in kindergarten, a Thursday in first grade, and so on until he had tasted the full range of primary school teaching experiences. The regular teachers of the classes where he was guest teacher for a day got to see their students and their setting from a new perspective. The cooperating teacher experienced a richer palette of challenges and satisfactions than teaching second grade allows. The children were revisited by their fondly remembered second grade teacher, or had a preview of what was to come in a year or two. And the sense of community and mutual understanding among the faculty was enhanced. Furthermore, this seems like excellent preparation for this teacher if he chooses to move on to a primary school principalship (head). And it didn't cost an extra penny, thanks to the presence of a student teacher.

The second story is set in a junior high school (12- to 14- year-olds). A woman who teaches history told me that she was able to revise, update and improve all of the tests and writing assignments that she will use next year with her history classes, using time freed by her student teacher. She admitted that she had intended to tackle this task for the past two years, but she simply did not have time to do so until the student teacher relieved her of three sections – half of her usual teaching load.

Another constructive way to organize the later weeks of student teaching is as *co-teaching*, with responsibility shared equally by veteran and novice. Co-teaching can be a delicate exercise in teamwork, in which the partners must be clear about what they hope to contribute to the whole and how they will manage transitions in leadership of the class. Co-teaching also provides chances for the veteran to see and feel the responses and sense-making activities of the children from a participant–observer perspective, which is rarely accessible when leading and managing a class, and also to move into and out of the perspectives of teacher, learner and colleague sharing a common agenda. As well, co-teaching can change the tone of planning and retrospective sessions away from threatening and one-sided evaluation, towards collaborative and mutually vulnerable conversation about teaching and learning from experience. Both teachers become learners, furthering their professional development and combining their strengths for the sake of the children.

ENERGY AND MORALE

'It's my *duty* to help new teachers get off to a good start.'

'It's great having a bright, young, energetic person around; it gives me hope for the future.'

'Most of my colleagues are within five or six years of retirement. We need to pass on all that we know about teaching before it's too late.'

'He reminds me of myself when I was a student teacher. I'm trying
to do as much for him as my mentor did for me 20 years ago.'
'When I did student teaching it was "sink or swim". Today, we're
doing a much more responsible job.'
'We couldn't have pulled off the field trip without this student
teacher's help.'

These are quotes and paraphrases of what veterans have told me about the
personal and relational side of working with student teachers. Their comments
reveal a sense of duty, dedication and idealism not often reflected in sociological
or popular literature about the profession. These are the voices of wise and
compassionate professionals who care about the future of schooling and about
the careers of those who follow in their footsteps. They also show that working
closely with a young, energetic, highly motivated student of teaching can be a
real morale booster. For few things make a teacher feel better than being listened
to, being conspicuously and immediately helpful, being valued, appreciated, and
imitated. These legitimate sources of satisfaction are much more likely to come
from close work with a student teacher than they are from secondary school
students or young children. The psychic rewards of teaching are too few and
fleeting for us to ignore the possibility that working with a student teacher can
rank high among them.

ANALYSIS OF TEACHING

By 'analysis of teaching' I do not mean to imply that veteran teachers should
become researchers on teaching as a consequence of working with beginners.
Rather, I want to make the case that working with a beginner can lead
cooperating teachers to ask new questions and revisit old questions about their
own practice; can move them to see themselves, their students, and the struggles
of a beginner in a new light; can, as the anthropologists say, 'make the familiar
strange' and reveal the remarkable in what has become ordinary.

One example of a fact about teaching that beginners remind veterans of
concerns the physical and psychological demands of teaching. Student teachers
typically find themselves exhausted and in mild shock after their first week of
teaching, with sore feet, bloodshot eyes, and a briefcase full of uncorrected
student work. They are amazed at the stamina of their older mentor, and
understandably nervous about meeting the demands of teaching, day in and day
out. For their part, the veterans are usually surprised at the fragile state of youth
today. But the virtue of being so vividly reminded of the taken for granted
demands of teaching should not be underestimated. For it is all too easy for an
experienced teacher to blame himself or herself for tiredness, feelings of lone-
liness and uncertainty, and for symptoms of stress when he or she forgets that
the very nature of the job of teacher falls somewhere near the intensity and
isolation level of an air traffic controller.

A related reminder to the veteran teacher concerns the prominent role of feelings and emotions in teaching and school learning. Experienced teachers and teacher-educators rarely remark on how emotion laden and volatile schooling can be. Social tension, mixed messages, control, conflict, fear, joy, exaltation, racism, bullying, assault, insult, injury, competition, cooperation, sensuality, love and grief – all these are swirling at or near the surface of virtually every primary and secondary school. Veteran teachers have learned to cope, to screen these emotions out, to talk of grade level performance in maths and reading, to steer clear of situations that might blow up, and to refer increasing numbers of children labelled 'emotionally disturbed' to specialists in behavioural control. But novices are not so wary, not so prudent, not so defended. They cry easily; their hearts bleed for the child excluded; they try too hard to make everything come out fairly and happily. And in so doing, they remind us all that the curriculum is deeper and wider and more morally complex to negotiate than we care to remember.

Beginners teach veterans about teaching in still another way: they beg to know *why* learning activities work, *why* the prescribed sequence of topics makes sense, *why* the classroom reward structure is organized as it is. In responding to these spoken and unspoken questions, the cooperating teacher listens to herself or himself, re-examines rationales old and new, and begins to articulate his or her own implicit theory of teaching and learning. We know that one of the most powerful ways to learn something is to teach it to another. This example of teaching about oneself, one's reasons, priorities and values, can increase precision and coherence in veteran teachers' personal theories and belief systems. To reveal something deep and important about ourselves clarifies and confirms who we are and why.

In closing, I want to consider some of the implications of looking at student teaching as a thought provoking learning experience for veterans. First, this view of learning from beginners affects the way we might recruit, relate to and collaborate with cooperating teachers. If only half of the potential benefits of working with beginners mentioned above are realized, teachers should be competing intensely for the honour. But I don't see that happening. How might teacher-educators rethink the ways in which we portray the role of mentor teacher, reform the ways in which we support and interact with them, and open our eyes to what university staff have to learn from a re-negotiated partnership with the field? I don't pretend to have the answers to these questions, but I think that they ought to be pursued directly and urgently as part of national conversations about reform of teacher education.

Second, the talks I have had with veteran teachers about their dealings with beginners have implications for the concept of 'teachers as teacher-educators'. One of the messages I take from these conversations is that experienced teachers are eager to do a first-class, contemporary job of helping prepare new teachers, but, at the same time, feel inadequately equipped to do so. Under these circumstances it is no surprise that teachers and university teacher-educators will continue to talk past one another and perpetuate the pitfalls of hit-or-miss learning from experience. What can we do to include cooperating teachers in the debates about how to improve teacher education? What transformations in their knowledge about learning to teach well are needed in order to teach a novice how to begin? And how can such 'metapedagogical content knowledge' be discovered and made widely available?

Finally, this exercise in thinking about learning from mentoring has broadened my understanding of the expression 'professional development'. Beyond in-service workshops, conferences and required postgraduate study, professional development can come to mean 'taking a meaningful part in the development of our profession'. One important and immediately available way for veteran teachers to play a part and have a voice is to become more involved in learning from beginners.

Afterword

On Cultivating Thoughtful Teaching

Looking back on the contents of this book, I have come to understand it as an unapologetically personal portrait of what I hold most dear about teachers and schoolchildren. While I have cited and borrowed from published writings and unpublished conversations with hundreds of teachers, students and researchers, in the end this is an autobiographical tale. But this autobiography has an activist agenda. In Vivian Paley's words,

> ... we all have the need to explain ourselves. Teachers seldom
> have the chance to do so ... My story, like anyone else's story, is a
> morality tale. You do not share your experience without the belief
> that there are lessons that have to be learned (1989, p. xv).

These lessons that must be learned are partly history lessons: about how teaching, learning and schooling looked, sounded, and felt to me, a hybrid teacher-researcher-parent-optimist. And they are partly lessons about alternative futures, for individual teachers and for all who can say 'I teach'.

Cultivating thoughtful teaching suggests a whole universe of possibilities to me. I am genuinely excited about these dreams and visions, about the fresh spirit of grassroots reform, the energizing projects, conversations, and collaborations that I imagine bursting forth among teachers who commit themselves to serious pursuit of the question 'what does it mean for us, here and now, to cultivate thoughtful teaching?'

But I am also realistic. I recognize that the lives of teachers and schoolchildren are complicated and constrained in many real ways (and in many significant but imaginary ways). The call to cultivate thoughtful teaching is also a call to sail in harm's way, to complicate your life even more, to forego some of the comfort that comes with unconsciousness, compliance with unexamined traditions, or retreat into cynicism. This is a call to raise expectations and risk disappointments.

In short, cultivating thoughtful teaching presents us with a true dilemma, which can never be solved once and for all. But dilemmas can be 'managed': you and I can take this one on, one day at a time, deciding in context where and how to advance our local, personal thoughtfulness agenda. We can decide which crusades we simply *must* embrace, and which issues are too hot to handle, too risky or expensive to engage right now, or ever. We can lead and we can follow, sometimes on the same day, for the sake of cultivating more thoughtful teaching.

This reminds me of the story of a distinguished family therapist. Families, like classrooms, are complex, dynamic social systems; much too complicated and emotion-charged to 'fix' or 'improve' through generic, abstract solutions. Instead, the therapist's approach has two parts: first, he joins the family where they are. He figuratively and literally moves into the family, to develop a felt sense of the whole family as a deeply and subtly connected system, to see and experience the family system from the points of view of all its different members. Second, as he comes to know the family in this intimate way, he asks himself this question again and again: what is *one small thing* that this family could change that might make its life more healthy, more adaptive? (Examples might include turning off the TV during the evening meal; entering by the front door rather than the back door; reactivating a long-dormant bedtime or morning ritual.) Invariably the therapist found that concentrating on one small change in a family's habits and interaction patterns had a ripple effect, leading to many other adjustments. Furthermore, the family felt relatively safe in agreeing to make only one small change: it was modest, reversible, cheap and not as overwhelming as the fear that an outside expert was going to force it to change *everything*.

Teachers of every kind are in a position that is a cross between that of the family therapist and of the head of household. Cultivating thoughtful teaching calls for looking, listening and feeling the school situation with respect for every point of view, and asking, again and again, what one small change we could try that is close to the heart of what matters most.

The journey towards thoughtful teaching cannot begin too soon. I urge prospective teachers and their teacher-educators to practise the sometimes awkward feeling work of learning how to invite and sustain authentic, two-way conversations about teaching, learning and life. Often these conversations are brief, accidental and even seen as digressions from the task-oriented business of teacher education. But, more and more often, thoughtful teacher-educators are beginning to experiment with ways to structure, organize and learn from authentic conversation groups of pre-service teachers (Florio-Ruane and deTar, 1995) and beginning teachers and veterans (Cavazos, 1994; Featherstone, Pfeiffer and Smith, 1993; Swidler, 1994). The briefest summary of what these teacher-researcher teams are learning is that authentic conversation, with its embedded personal stories, is a powerful yet challenging way to make sense of experience; to remember, reinterpret and reorganize personal and social knowledge; to give and receive the support we all need to sustain ourselves and pursue our own visions and ideals.

If I had but one small change to propose to the family of school teachers it would be this: begin a Thoughtful Teaching Circle, in which four to six teachers come together voluntarily once a week or twice a month to talk, to listen, to learn from one another; to give support to each other, and advice only when asked. The variations on this form are endless, from book clubs reading the same books, to child study groups, to action research teams, curriculum design and redesign, and video, film and drama outings and discussions. The best ones I know of all include food, comfortable surroundings, laughter, a focus on doing something of meaningful common interest outside the group's meeting times, and a shared commitment to doing right for schoolchildren and for themselves. Beyond this, as it should, thoughtful teaching takes on a life of its own.

East Lansing, Michigan
13 October 1994

Bibliography

Anderson, L. M. and Evertson, C. M. (1978, February) Classroom organization at the beginning of school: Two case studies. Paper presented to the American Association of Colleges for Teacher Education, Chicago.

Baker, E. L. (1984, March) Can educational research inform educational practice? Yes! *Phi Delta Kappan*, **65**:453–5.

Ball, D. L. and Wilson, S. (1993, June) Integrity in teaching. Paper presented to the Conference on Teacher Knowledge, Tel Aviv University, Tel Aviv, Israel.

Ball, D. L. (1986, September) Unlearning to teach mathematics. Paper presented at the meeting of the North American Chapter of the International Group for the Psychology of Mathematics Education, East Lansing, Michigan.

Ball, D. L. and Feiman-Nemser, S. (1986) *The Use of Curricular Materials: What Beginning Elementary Teachers Learn and What they Need to Know* (Research Series No. 174). East Lansing: Michigan State University, Institute for Research on Teaching.

Berlak, A. and Berlak, H. (1981) *Dilemmas of Schooling: Teaching and Social Change*. London: Methuen & Co.

Berliner, D. C. and Carter, K. J. (1986, October) Differences in processing classroom information by expert and novice teachers. Paper presented to the International Study Association on Teacher Thinking, Leuven, Belgium.

Brophy, J. E. and Good, T. L. (1974) *Teacher-Student Relationships: Causes and Consequences*. New York: Holt, Rinehart and Winston.

Brophy, J. E. and Good, T. L. (1986) Teacher behavior and student achievement. In M. C. Wittrock (ed.), *Handbook of Research on Teaching*, Third Edition. New York: Macmillan, 328–75.

Buckley, P. K. and Cooper, J. M. (1978, March) An ethnographic study of an elementary school teacher's establishment and maintenance of group norms. Paper presented at the annual meeting of the American Educational Research Association, Toronto.

Bussis, A. M., Chittenden, E. and Amarel, M. (1976) *Beyond Surface Curriculum*. Boulder, CO: Westview Press.

Calderhead, J. (1983, April) Research into teachers' and student teachers' cognitions: Exploring the nature of classroom practice. Paper presented at the annual meeting of the American Educational Research Association, Montreal.

Campbell, J., with Moyers, B. (1988) *The Power of Myth*. New York: Doubleday.

Carnahan, R. S. (1980) *The Effects of Teacher Planning on Classroom Process* (Tech. Rep. No. 541). Madison: Wisconsin R & D Center for Individualized Schooling.

Carroll, J. B. (1963) A model of school learning. *Teachers College Record*, **64**: 723–33.

Cavazos, L. M. (1994) A search for missing voices: A narrative inquiry into the lives of women science teachers. Unpublished doctoral dissertation, Michigan State University.

Clandinin, D. J. (1986) *Classroom Practice: Teacher Images in Action*. London: Falmer Press.

Clandinin, J. and Connelly, F. M. (1984) Personal practical knowledge at Bay Street School: Ritual, personal philosophy and image. In R. Halkes and J. Olson (eds), *Teacher Thinking: A New Perspective on Persisting Problems in Education* (pp. 134–48). Lisse, The Netherlands: Swets & Zeitlinger.

Clark, C. M. (1983) Research on teacher planning: An inventory of the knowledge base. In D. C. Smith (ed.), *Essential Knowledge for Beginning Educators*. Washington D.C.: American Association of Colleges for Teacher Education, 5–15.

Clark, C. M. (1990) The teacher and the taught: Moral transactions in the classroom. In J. I. Goodlad, R. Soder and K. A. Sirotnik (eds), *The Moral Dimensions of Teaching*. San Francisco: Jossey-Bass, 251–65.

Clark, C. M. and Elmore, J. L. (1979) *Teacher Planning in the First Weeks of School* (Research Series No. 56). East Lansing: Michigan State University, Institute for Research on Teaching.

Clark, C. M. and Elmore, J. L. (1981) *Transforming Curriculum in Mathematics, Science, and Writing: A Case Study of Teacher Yearly Planning* (Research Series No. 99). East Lansing: Michigan State University, Institute for Research on Teaching.

Clark, C. M. and Florio, S., with Elmore, J. L., Martin, J., Maxwell, R. J. and Metheny, W. (1982) *Understanding Writing in School: A Descriptive Case Study of Writing and its Instruction in Two Classrooms* (Research Series No. 104). East Lansing: Institute for Research on Teaching, Michigan State University.

Clark, C. M. and Lampert, M. (1986) The study of teacher thinking: Implications for teacher education. *Journal of Teacher Education*, **37** (5):27–31.

Clark, C. M. and Peterson, P. L. (1986) Teachers' thought processes. In M. Wittrock (ed.), *Handbook of Research on Teaching*, Third Edition. New York: Macmillan, 255–96.

Clark, C. M. and Yinger, R. J. (1979) *Three Studies of Teacher Planning* (Research Series No. 55). East Lansing: Michigan State University, Institute for Research on Teaching.

Conners, R. D. (1978) An Analysis of teacher thought processes, beliefs, and principles during instruction. Unpublished doctoral dissertation, University of Alberta, Edmonton, Canada.

Cronbach, L. J. (1975) Beyond the two disciplines of scientific psychology. *American Psychologist*, **30**:116–26.

Csikszentmihalyi, M. and Larson, R. (1984) *Being Adolescent: Conflict and Growth in the Teenage Years*. New York: Basic Books.

Doyle, W. (1977) Learning the classroom environment: An ecological analysis. *Journal of Teacher Education*, **28** (6): 51–5.

Doyle, W. (1979) Making managerial decisions in classrooms. In D. L. Duke (ed.), *Classroom Management* (78th yearbook of the National Society for the Study of Education, Part 2, pp. 42–74). Chicago: University of Chicago Press.

Doyle, W. (1983) Academic work. *Review of Educational Research*, **53**: 159–99.

Dreyfus, H. I. and Dreyfus, S. E. (1990) What is morality? A phenomenological account of the development of ethical expertise. In D. Rasmussen (ed.), *Universalism vs. Communitarianism: Contemporary Debate in Ethics*. Cambridge, MA: The MIT Press, 237–64.

Duffy, G. (1977, December) A study of teacher conceptions of reading. Paper presented at the National Reading Conference, New Orleans.

Eisner, E. W. (1984) Can educational research inform educational practice? *Phi Delta Kappan*, **65** (March): 447–52.

Elbaz, F. (1981) The teacher's 'practical knowledge': Report of a case study. *Curriculum Inquiry*, **11**: 43–71.

Featherstone, H., Pfeiffer, L. C. and Smith, S. P. (1993) *Learning in Good Company: Report on a Pilot Study*. East Lansing: NCRTL Research Report 93–2.

Fenstermacher, G. D. (1979) A philosophical consideration of recent research on teacher effectiveness. In L. S. Shulman (ed.), *Review of Research in Education*, **6**: 157–85. Itasca, IL: F. E. Peacock.

Fisher, C. W., Berliner, D. C., Filby, N. N., Marliave, R., Cahen, L. S. and Dishaw, M. M. (1980) Teaching behaviors, academic learning time, and student achievement: An overview. In C. Denham and A. Lieberman (eds), *Time to Learn*, 7–32. Washington, D.C.: National Institute of Education.

Floden, R. E. and Feiman, S. (1981) Should teachers be taught to be rational? *Journal of Education for Teachers*, **7**: 274–83.

Florio, S. and Clark, C. M. (1982) The functions of writing in an elementary classroom. *Research in the Teaching of English*, **16**: 115–30.

Florio-Ruane, S. and deTar, J. (1995) Conflict and consensus in teacher candidates' discussion of ethnic autobiography. *English Education*, **27**(1), 11–39.

Goodlad, J. I., Soder, R. and Sirotnik, K. A. (eds) (1990) *The Moral Dimensions of Teaching*. San Francisco: Jossey-Bass.

Grant, G. (1988) *Teaching Critical Thinking*. New York: Praeger.

Grant, G. (1991) Ways of constructing classroom meaning: Two stories about knowing and seeing. *Journal of Curriculum Studies*, **23**(5): 397–408.

Gudmundsdottir, S. (1989) *Knowledge use among Experienced Teachers: Four Case Studies of High School Teaching*. Unpublished doctoral dissertation, Stanford University.

Gudmundsdottir, S. (1991) Ways of seeing are ways of knowing: the pedagogical content knowledge of an expert English teacher. *Journal of Curriculum Studies*, **23**(5) 409–21.

Hall, S. and Grant, G. (1991) On what is known and seen: A conversation with a research participant. *Journal of Curriculum Studies*, **23**(5): 423–8.

Hill, J., Yinger, R. J. and Robbins, D. (1981, April) Instructional planning in a developmental preschool. Paper presented at the annual meeting of the American Educational Research Association, Los Angeles.

Housner, L. D. and Griffey, D. C. (1983, April) Teacher cognition: Differences in planning and interactive decision making between experienced and inexperienced teachers. Paper presented at the annual meeting of the American Educational Research Association, Montreal.

Ignatovich, F. R., Cusick, P. A. and Ray, J. E. (1979) *Value / Belief Patterns of Teachers and those Administrators Engaged in Attempts to Influence Teaching* (Research Series No. 43). East Lansing: Michigan State University, Institute for Research on Teaching.

Kounin, J. (1970) *Discipline and Group Management in Classrooms*. New York: Holt, Rinehart and Winston.

Kroma, S. (1983) Personal practical knowledge of language in teaching: An ethnographic study. Unpublished doctoral dissertation, University of Toronto.

Kuhs, T. (1980) Teachers' conceptions of mathematics. Unpublished doctoral dissertation, Michigan State University, East Lansing.

Kundera, M. (1982) *The Joke*, translated from the Czech by Michael Henry Heim. New York: Harper & Row.

Lampert, M. (1984) Teaching about thinking and thinking about teaching. *Journal of Curriculum Studies*, **16**: 1–18.

Lampert, M. (1985) How do teachers manage to teach? Perspectives on problems in practice. *Harvard Educational Review*, **55**: 178–94.

Leinhardt, G. and Greeno, J. (1984) The cognitive skill of teaching. Paper presented at the annual meeting of the American Educational Research Association, Montreal, Canada.

Levi-Strauss, C. (1967) *The Scope of Anthropology*. London: Cape.

Lundgren, U. P. (1972) *Frame Factors and the Teaching Process*. Stockholm: Almqvist and Wiksell.

Marland, P. W. (1977) A Study of teachers' interactive thoughts. Unpublished doctoral dissertation, University of Alberta, Edmonton, Canada.

McConaghy, J. (1991) Teachers' stories and pedagogical insights. Unpublished doctoral dissertation, University of Alberta.

McLeod, M. A. (1981) The identification of intended learning outcomes by early childhood teachers: An exploratory study. Unpublished doctoral dissertation, University of Alberta, Edmonton, Canada.

Melville, H. (1851; 1976 edn) *Moby Dick or, The Whale*. New York: W. W. Norton & Co.

Miller, A. (1982) *The Drama of the Gifted Child*. New York: Basic Books.

Miller, A. (1983) *For Your Own Good: Hidden Cruelty in Child-Rearing and the Roots of Violence*. New York: Farar, Straus and Giroux.

Miller, A. (1984) *Thou Shalt not be Aware: Society's Betrayal of the Child*. New York: New American Library.

Miller, A. (1986) *Pictures of a Childhood*. New York: Farrar, Straus and Giroux.

Miller, A. (1990) *Banished Knowledge: Facing Childhood Injuries*. New York: Doubleday.

Miller, A. (1990) *The Untouched Key: Tracing Childhood Trauma in Creativity and Destructiveness*. New York: Doubleday.

Morine, G. and Vallance, E. (1975) *Special Study B: A Study of Teacher and Pupil Perceptions of Classroom Interaction* (Tech. Rep. No. 75–11–6). San Francisco: Far West Laboratory.

Morine-Dershimer, G. and Vallance, E. (1976) *Teacher Planning* (Beginning Teacher Evaluation Study, Special Report C). San Francisco: Far West Laboratory.

Munby, H. (1983, April) A qualitative study of teachers' beliefs and principles. Paper presented at the annual meeting of the American Educational Research Association, Montreal.

Neale, D. C., Pace, A. J. and Case, A. B. (1983, April) The influence of training, experience, and organizational environment on teachers' use of the systematic planning model. Paper presented at the annual meeting of the American Educational Research Association, Montreal, Canada.

Niemeyer, R. and Moon, A. (1986, April) Researching decision-making in the supervision of student teachers. Paper presented at the annual meeting of the American Educational Research Association, San Francisco, CA.

Nisbett, R. E. and Ross, L. (1980) *Human Inference: Strategies and Shortcomings of Social Judgment*. Englewood Cliffs, NJ: Prentice-Hall.

Olson, J. K. (1981) Teacher influence in the classroom. *Instructional Science*, 10: 259–75.

Paine, L. W. (1986, October) Teaching as a virtuoso performance: The model and its consequences for teacher thinking and preparation in China. Paper presented to the Conference on Teacher Thinking and Professional Action, International Study Association on Teacher Thinking, Leuven, Belgium.

Paley, V. G. (1989) *White Teacher*. Cambridge, MA: Harvard University Press.

Pater, W. (1907) *Marius the Epicurean: His Sensations and Ideals*, Vol. 2. London: Macmillan.

Peterson, P. L. and Clark, C. M. (1978) Teachers' reports of their cognitive processes during teaching. *American Educational Research Journal*, 15: 555–65.

Peterson, P. L., Marx, R. W. and Clark, C. M. (1978) Teacher planning, teacher behavior, and student achievement. *American Educational Research Journal* 15: 417–32.

Philips, S. U. (1972) Participation structures and communicative competence: Warm Springs children in community and classroom. In C. B. Cazden, V. John and D. Hymes (eds), *Functions of Language in the Classroom*, 370–94. New York: Teachers College Press.

Phillips, D. C. (1980) What do the researcher and the practitioner have to offer each other? *Educational Researcher*, 9: 17–24.

Porter, A. C. (1986) *Collaborating with Teachers on Research: Pioneering Efforts at the Institute for Research on Teaching* (Occasional Paper No. 105). East Lansing: Michigan State University, Institute for Research on Teaching.

Posner, G. J., Strike, K. A. Hewson, P.W. and Gertzog, W. A. (1982) Accommodation of a scientific conception: Toward a theory of conceptual change. *Science Education*, **66**: 211–27.

Richardson, E. S. (1964) *In the Early World*. Wellington, New Zealand: New Zealand Council of Educational Research.

Roth, K. J. (1985) Conceptual change learning and student processing of science texts. Unpublished doctoral dissertation, Michigan State University.

Roth, K. J. Smith, E. L. and Anderson, C. W. (1983, April) Students' conceptions of photosynthesis and food for plants. Paper presented at the annual meeting of the American Educational Research Association, Montreal.

Rowe, M. B. (1974) Wait time and rewards as instructional variables, their influence on language, logic, and fate control: Part one–wait time. *Journal of Research in Science Teaching*, **11**: 81–94.

Rust, F. (1986) Supervisors' conceptions of their role: A journal-based study. Paper presented at the annual meeting of the American Educational Research Association, San Francisco.

Schon, D. (1983) *The Reflective Practitioner: How Professionals Think in Action*. New York: Basic Books.

Shavelson, R. J. and Stern, P. (1981) Research on teachers' pedagogical thoughts, judgments, decisions, and behavior. *Review of Educational Research*, **51**: 455–98.

Shulman, L. S. (1984, Autumn) It's harder to teach in class than to be a physician. *Stanford School of Education News*, p. 3.

Shulman, L. S. (1987) Knowledge and teaching: Foundations of the new reform. *Harvard Educational Review*, **57** (1): 1–22.

Shultz, J. and Florio, S. (1979) Stop and freeze: The negotiation of social and physical space in a kindergarten/first grade classroom. *Anthropology and Education Quarterly*, **10**: 166–81.

Shultz, J., Florio, S. and Erickson, F. (1982) Where's the floor? Aspects of the cultural organization of social relationships in communication at home and at school. In P. Gilmore and A. Glatthorn (eds), *Children In and Out of School: Ethnography and Education*, 88–123. Washington, D.C.: Center for Applied Linguistics.

Simon, A. and Boyer, E. G. (eds) (1970) Mirrors for behavior II: An anthology of observational instruments. *Classroom Interaction Newsletter*, special edition.

Simon, H. A. (1957) *Models of Man*. New York: Wiley.

Smith, M. L. and Shepard, L. A. (1988) Kindergarten readiness and retention: A qualitative study of teachers' beliefs and practices. *American Educational Research Journal*, **25**: 307–33.

Sockett, H. (1993) *The Moral Base for Teacher Professionalism*. New York: Teachers College Press.

Swidler, S. (1994, February) Discursive congruence in storytelling: Modal conventions in a democratic teachers' support group. Paper presented to the Urban Ethnography Forum, University of Pennsylvania, Philadelphia, PA.

Tikunoff, W. J. and Ward, B. A. (1978) *A Naturalistic Study of the Initiation of Students into Three Classroom Social Systems* (Report A-78-11). San Francisco: Far West Laboratory.

Tom, A. (1984) *Teaching as a Moral Craft*. New York: Longman.

Wagner, A. (1984) Conflicts in consciousness: Imperative cognitions can lead to knots in thinking. In R. Halkes and J. Olson (eds), *Teacher Thinking: A new Perspective on Persisting Problems in Education* (pp. 163–75). Lisse, The Netherlands: Swets and Zietlinger.

Wilson, S. M., Shulman, L. S. and Richert, A. (1987) '150 different ways' of knowing. In J. Calderhead (ed.) *Exploring Teacher Thinking*. London: Cassell, 104–24.

Yinger, R. J. (1977) A study of teacher planning: Description and theory development using ethnographic and information processing methods. Unpublished doctoral dissertation, Michigan State University, East Lansing.

Yinger, R. J. (1979) Routines in teacher planning. *Theory into Practice*, **18**: 163–9.

Yinger, R. J. (1987) Learning the language of practice. *Curriculum Inquiry* **17**: 3, 293–318.

Zeuli, J. (1994) How do teachers understand research when they read it? *Teaching and Teacher Education*, **10** (1), 39–55.

Name Index

Subject Index